Proper Education Group

4 Practice Tests for the Pennsylvania Real Estate Exam

"The secret to getting ahead is getting started."
Mark Twain

Copyright © 2019 Proper Education Group. All rights reserved.
Printed in the United States of America.

Proper Education books may be purchased for educational, business, or sales promotional use. For more information, contact our corporate / institutional sales department: contact@propereducation.group
No part of this publication may be reproduced, stored in a retrieval system, or transmitted in any form or by means electronic, mechanical, photocopying, or otherwise, without prior written permission of the publisher.

Proper Education Group

Table of Contents

Introduction 1
   1.1 Requirements 1
   1.2 About the Exam 1
   1.3 How to Apply 2
   1.4 Exam Results 2

Practice Test 1 3
   National Portion 7
   State Portion 17
   Answer Key – National Portion 25
   Answer Key – State Portion 37

Practice Test 2 43
   National Portion 47
   State Portion 57
   Answer Key – National Portion 65
   Answer Key – State Portion 77

Practice Test 3 83
   National Portion 87
   State Portion 97
   Answer Key – National Portion 105
   Answer Key – State Portion 117

Practice Test 4 123
   National Portion 127
   State Portion 137
   Answer Key – National Portion 145
   Answer Key – State Portion 157

Resources 163
   3.1 Finding a broker 163
   3.2 Interviewing 164

Introduction

1.1 Requirements

In order to qualify to take the test, you must take the 75-hour pre-licensing curriculum.

On the day of the test, you must bring the following:

1. Valid and not expired government-issued ID. Bring one of the things listed below:
    a. Driver's license
    b. State issued identification (ex. non-driver ID)
    c. United States Passport
2. A second ID that contains your signature and legal name

You are not required to bring a calculator, but you are **highly encouraged to do so** as there will be simple mathematical questions that require multiplication and division. Do not rely on the one on your phone because **phones will not be allowed**.

1.2 About the Exam

The test is 180 minutes long and composed of two sections.

The national portion is composed of 80 multiple choice questions and the time limit is 120 minutes. You must answer at least 60 of 80 questions correctly to pass the national portion.

Introduction

The state portion is composed of 30 multiple choice questions and the time limit is 60 minutes. You must answer at least 23 of 30 questions correctly to pass the state portion.

The exam is administered through a computer.

1.3 How to Apply

To apply for the exam, visit the Pennsylvania Department of State website and submit the required the forms:

https://www.dos.pa.gov/ProfessionalLicensing/BoardsCommissions/RealEstateCommission/Pages/Salesperson-Applications.aspx

All of the official documentation pertaining payments, documents, and forms can be found there.

1.4 Exam Results

Your score will be given to you immediately after finishing the exam.

Practice Test 1

Directions:

1. You have a 120-minute time limit for the national portion, and a 60-minute time limit for the state portion.

2. To pass, you must answer at least 60 out of 80 questions correctly on the national portion **AND** at least 23 out of 30 questions on the state portion.

3. Some questions will require mathematics. You may use a calculator.

4. **Phones and pagers are not allowed. Having either will result in automatic dismissal from the exam and nullification of exam scores.**

Tips:

- Answer all questions even if you are unsure.
- Mark any questions you are stuck on and revisit them after you are done. The exam is timed so make sure you finish as many questions as you can.
- After reading the question, try answering it in your head first to avoid getting confused by the choices.
- Read the entire question before looking at the answers.
- Use the process of elimination to filter out choices that don't seem correct to increase your chances of selecting the correct answer.
- Be aware of important keywords like **not, sometimes, always,** and **never**. These words completely alter the ask of the question so it's important to keep track of them.

PLEASE READ THESE INSTRUCTIONS CAREFULLY.

Practice Test 1

Name: _____   Date: _____

NATIONAL PORTION

1. Ⓐ Ⓑ Ⓒ Ⓓ	31. Ⓐ Ⓑ Ⓒ Ⓓ	61. Ⓐ Ⓑ Ⓒ Ⓓ	
2. Ⓐ Ⓑ Ⓒ Ⓓ	32. Ⓐ Ⓑ Ⓒ Ⓓ	62. Ⓐ Ⓑ Ⓒ Ⓓ	
3. Ⓐ Ⓑ Ⓒ Ⓓ	33. Ⓐ Ⓑ Ⓒ Ⓓ	63. Ⓐ Ⓑ Ⓒ Ⓓ	
4. Ⓐ Ⓑ Ⓒ Ⓓ	34. Ⓐ Ⓑ Ⓒ Ⓓ	64. Ⓐ Ⓑ Ⓒ Ⓓ	
5. Ⓐ Ⓑ Ⓒ Ⓓ	35. Ⓐ Ⓑ Ⓒ Ⓓ	65. Ⓐ Ⓑ Ⓒ Ⓓ	
6. Ⓐ Ⓑ Ⓒ Ⓓ	36. Ⓐ Ⓑ Ⓒ Ⓓ	66. Ⓐ Ⓑ Ⓒ Ⓓ	
7. Ⓐ Ⓑ Ⓒ Ⓓ	37. Ⓐ Ⓑ Ⓒ Ⓓ	67. Ⓐ Ⓑ Ⓒ Ⓓ	
8. Ⓐ Ⓑ Ⓒ Ⓓ	38. Ⓐ Ⓑ Ⓒ Ⓓ	68. Ⓐ Ⓑ Ⓒ Ⓓ	
9. Ⓐ Ⓑ Ⓒ Ⓓ	39. Ⓐ Ⓑ Ⓒ Ⓓ	69. Ⓐ Ⓑ Ⓒ Ⓓ	
10. Ⓐ Ⓑ Ⓒ Ⓓ	40. Ⓐ Ⓑ Ⓒ Ⓓ	70. Ⓐ Ⓑ Ⓒ Ⓓ	
11. Ⓐ Ⓑ Ⓒ Ⓓ	41. Ⓐ Ⓑ Ⓒ Ⓓ	71. Ⓐ Ⓑ Ⓒ Ⓓ	
12. Ⓐ Ⓑ Ⓒ Ⓓ	42. Ⓐ Ⓑ Ⓒ Ⓓ	72. Ⓐ Ⓑ Ⓒ Ⓓ	
13. Ⓐ Ⓑ Ⓒ Ⓓ	43. Ⓐ Ⓑ Ⓒ Ⓓ	73. Ⓐ Ⓑ Ⓒ Ⓓ	
14. Ⓐ Ⓑ Ⓒ Ⓓ	44. Ⓐ Ⓑ Ⓒ Ⓓ	74. Ⓐ Ⓑ Ⓒ Ⓓ	
15. Ⓐ Ⓑ Ⓒ Ⓓ	45. Ⓐ Ⓑ Ⓒ Ⓓ	75. Ⓐ Ⓑ Ⓒ Ⓓ	
16. Ⓐ Ⓑ Ⓒ Ⓓ	46. Ⓐ Ⓑ Ⓒ Ⓓ	76. Ⓐ Ⓑ Ⓒ Ⓓ	
17. Ⓐ Ⓑ Ⓒ Ⓓ	47. Ⓐ Ⓑ Ⓒ Ⓓ	77. Ⓐ Ⓑ Ⓒ Ⓓ	
18. Ⓐ Ⓑ Ⓒ Ⓓ	48. Ⓐ Ⓑ Ⓒ Ⓓ	78. Ⓐ Ⓑ Ⓒ Ⓓ	
19. Ⓐ Ⓑ Ⓒ Ⓓ	49. Ⓐ Ⓑ Ⓒ Ⓓ	79. Ⓐ Ⓑ Ⓒ Ⓓ	
20. Ⓐ Ⓑ Ⓒ Ⓓ	50. Ⓐ Ⓑ Ⓒ Ⓓ	80. Ⓐ Ⓑ Ⓒ Ⓓ	
21. Ⓐ Ⓑ Ⓒ Ⓓ	51. Ⓐ Ⓑ Ⓒ Ⓓ		
22. Ⓐ Ⓑ Ⓒ Ⓓ	52. Ⓐ Ⓑ Ⓒ Ⓓ		
23. Ⓐ Ⓑ Ⓒ Ⓓ	53. Ⓐ Ⓑ Ⓒ Ⓓ		
24. Ⓐ Ⓑ Ⓒ Ⓓ	54. Ⓐ Ⓑ Ⓒ Ⓓ		
25. Ⓐ Ⓑ Ⓒ Ⓓ	55. Ⓐ Ⓑ Ⓒ Ⓓ		
26. Ⓐ Ⓑ Ⓒ Ⓓ	56. Ⓐ Ⓑ Ⓒ Ⓓ		
27. Ⓐ Ⓑ Ⓒ Ⓓ	57. Ⓐ Ⓑ Ⓒ Ⓓ		
28. Ⓐ Ⓑ Ⓒ Ⓓ	58. Ⓐ Ⓑ Ⓒ Ⓓ		
29. Ⓐ Ⓑ Ⓒ Ⓓ	59. Ⓐ Ⓑ Ⓒ Ⓓ		
30. Ⓐ Ⓑ Ⓒ Ⓓ	60. Ⓐ Ⓑ Ⓒ Ⓓ		

Practice Test 1

Name: _____   Date: _____

STATE PORTION

1. Ⓐ Ⓑ Ⓒ Ⓓ
2. Ⓐ Ⓑ Ⓒ Ⓓ
3. Ⓐ Ⓑ Ⓒ Ⓓ
4. Ⓐ Ⓑ Ⓒ Ⓓ
5. Ⓐ Ⓑ Ⓒ Ⓓ
6. Ⓐ Ⓑ Ⓒ Ⓓ
7. Ⓐ Ⓑ Ⓒ Ⓓ
8. Ⓐ Ⓑ Ⓒ Ⓓ
9. Ⓐ Ⓑ Ⓒ Ⓓ
10. Ⓐ Ⓑ Ⓒ Ⓓ
11. Ⓐ Ⓑ Ⓒ Ⓓ
12. Ⓐ Ⓑ Ⓒ Ⓓ
13. Ⓐ Ⓑ Ⓒ Ⓓ
14. Ⓐ Ⓑ Ⓒ Ⓓ
15. Ⓐ Ⓑ Ⓒ Ⓓ
16. Ⓐ Ⓑ Ⓒ Ⓓ
17. Ⓐ Ⓑ Ⓒ Ⓓ
18. Ⓐ Ⓑ Ⓒ Ⓓ
19. Ⓐ Ⓑ Ⓒ Ⓓ
20. Ⓐ Ⓑ Ⓒ Ⓓ
21. Ⓐ Ⓑ Ⓒ Ⓓ
22. Ⓐ Ⓑ Ⓒ Ⓓ
23. Ⓐ Ⓑ Ⓒ Ⓓ
24. Ⓐ Ⓑ Ⓒ Ⓓ
25. Ⓐ Ⓑ Ⓒ Ⓓ
26. Ⓐ Ⓑ Ⓒ Ⓓ
27. Ⓐ Ⓑ Ⓒ Ⓓ
28. Ⓐ Ⓑ Ⓒ Ⓓ
29. Ⓐ Ⓑ Ⓒ Ⓓ
30. Ⓐ Ⓑ Ⓒ Ⓓ

National Portion

1. When applying for a loan, what is a **fixed rate**?

   A. A loan that has a predetermined repayment interest rate
   B. A loan that has an interest rate that varies over time
   C. A loan that accrues no interest
   D. A loan that pays off the interest before the principal

2. What act prohibits discrimination based on race or color?

   A. Fair Housing Act
   B. Civil Rights Act of 1866
   C. Civil Right Act of 1964
   D. Civil Rights Act Amendment of 1974

3. What is the financial document that contains a written promise to fulfill a certain payment?

   A. Invoice
   B. Promissory note
   C. Pro forma statement
   D. IOU

4. What is the term used to describe the act of replacing an existing mortgage with another?

   A. Refinancing
   B. Defaulting
   C. Foreclosure
   D. Reinvesting

5. Which is **not** an appurtenant right?

   A. Furnace
   B. Swimming pool
   C. Air conditioning
   D. All of the above

6. What is the name given to the banking option that allows a customer to deposit a specified amount for a predetermined period of time?

   A. Certificate of occupation
   B. Certificate of deposit
   C. Investment clause
   D. Mortgage

7. If a seller nets $225,000 after paying a 10% fee, what was the total he received?

   A. $202,500
   B. $224,990
   C. $250,000
   D. None of the above

8. What is the name given to the rate earned for borrowing or an investment per year?

   A. Rate lock
   B. Fixed rate
   C. Floating rate
   D. Annual percentage rate

9. Other than buying a home using traditional channels, what other methods can a prospective owner use to buy a home?

   A. Public auctions
   B. Tender
   C. Lease
   D. Escalation clause

10. What is the reviewing of a borrower's credit worthiness prior to loan approval?

    A. Buydown
    B. Pre-qualification
    C. Credit score
    D. Under qualification

11. What is the document that is used to transfer legal rights to act in the interest of a person?

    A. Disclosure form
    B. Power of attorney
    C. Pro forma statement
    D. Deed

12. What type of listing only guarantees commission for a sale within a specified period?

    A. Exclusive listing
    B. Net listing
    C. Single agency listing
    D. Multi agency listing

13. What type of brokerage mandates that the broker acts in the best interest of the buyer?

    A. Single agency
    B. Dual agency
    C. Multi agency
    D. Full service

14. What is the name of a transaction where both the buyer and seller are seeking the best deal?

    A. Real estate transaction
    B. Credit transaction
    C. Arms-length transaction
    D. Debited transaction

15. What is the name given to modification of billing calculation dates?

    A. Modified date
    B. Closing date
    C. Opening date
    D. Adjustment date

16. What is the name of the mortgage that is transferred by the seller to the buyer?

    A. Assumable mortgage
    B. Adjusted rate mortgage
    C. Fixed rate mortgage
    D. Floating mortgage

17. What is the contract that secures a future transaction?

    A. Deed
    B. Call option
    C. Title
    D. None of the above

18. What does an exclusive listing contract need to be considered valid?

    A. A net listing
    B. A commission rate of at least 6%
    C. A specified expiration date
    D. The signature of the grantee

19. What is it when another state recognizes your Pennsylvania real estate license?

    A. Transfer
    B. Limited basis policy
    C. Reciprocity
    D. None of the above

20. Which of the following is **not** a fiduciary duty?

    A. Accounting
    B. Confidentiality
    C. Obedience
    D. Privacy

21. What are contingencies as used in real estate?

    A. Conditions that must be met by both the buyer and the seller before closing
    B. Conditions set by the government on buying a home
    C. Conditions set by the bank in order to approve a loan for a mortgage
    D. Conditions that must be met to avoid judicial foreclosure

22. Who is a co-borrower?

    A. Any individual whose name appears on the loan document
    B. Someone that borrows money at the same time with you
    C. The mortgage broker that originates the loan for you
    D. An individual that guarantees your loan

23. What is the name given to a loan taken out to finance construction?

    A. Mortgage
    B. Construction loan
    C. Business loan
    D. Personal loan

24. What is the name given to the inspection done by the buyer before closing?

    A. Final inspection
    B. Advertorial
    C. Housing ratio
    D. Final walkthrough

Practice Test 1 – National Portion

25. What is the name given to a mortgage whose interest rate does **not** change throughout the payment period?

    A. Adjustable mortgage rate
    B. Floating rate
    C. Fixed mortgage rate
    D. Bridge loan

26. What is defined as the percentage owned by the buyer after making a down payment?

    A. Housing ratio
    B. Debt to income ratio
    C. Loan to value ratio
    D. Floating rate

27. What is the cash on cash return of a $60,000 investment that generates $1,000 in monthly cash flow?

    A. 1.67%
    B. 2%
    C. 20%
    D. None of the above

28. What is the term used to refer to the responsibility one individual has for the acts of another?

    A. Vicarious liability
    B. Fixed liability
    C. Current liability
    D. Contingent

29. What is the name given to a form used to explain the role of an agent in a real estate transaction?

    A. Purchase agreement
    B. Accountability
    C. Assignment contract
    D. Agency disclosure statement

30. A number of Pennsylvania brokers agreed on a set standard commission. What antitrust law are they guilty of violating?

    A. Commingling
    B. Price fixing
    C. Steering
    D. Discussing

31. Which government agency is responsible for determining the status of an independent contractor?

    A. Federal government
    B. Bank
    C. Department of State
    D. IRS

32. What is the nature of the title issued in condo ownership?

    A. Freehold
    B. Regular
    C. Deed
    D. Clear title

33. Mr. and Mrs. Johnson made a $350,000 profit on the sale of their primary home. How much do they owe in capital gains tax?

    A. $0
    B. $3,500
    C. $50,000
    D. Half of the amount earned

34. What is the status of an agent's license once it is revoked?

    A. Pending
    B. Cancelled
    C. Breached
    D. Suspended

35. Which insurance policy provides extra liability coverage for the insured party?

    A. Umbrella policy
    B. Home insurance
    C. Flood insurance
    D. Hazard insurance

36. What is never included in the process of valuation?

    A. Comparative Market Analysis
    B. Appraisal
    C. Location
    D. Condition of the house

37. What type of contract allows the parties involved to disaffirm without liability?

    A. Bilateral contract
    B. Implied contract
    C. Unilateral contract
    D. Voidable Contract

38. What fiduciary duty does a broker neglect by failing to disclosing the buyer's inability to afford a down payment?

    A. Obedience
    B. Disclosure
    C. Accountability
    D. Confidentiality

39. James and Peter co-own a property where they both have equal undivided interests and right of survivorship. What co-ownership agreement do they have?

    A. Tenancy in entirety
    B. Joint tenancy
    C. Tenancy in common
    D. Tenancy at will

40. What is an exclusive term to describe the lease entered when an individual buys shares from a housing corporation?

    A. Percentage lease
    B. Gross lease
    C. Net lease
    D. Proprietary lease

Practice Test 1 – National Portion

41. What is the state of having no legal effect?

    A. Enforceable
    B. Cancelled
    C. Void
    D. Terminated

42. How many square feet constitute an acre?

    A. 25,235
    B. 43,560
    C. 50,525
    D. 70,000

43. What is the set minimum amp for a new construction?

    A. 100 amps
    B. 150 amps
    C. 200 amps
    D. 250 amps

44. What is the debt-to-equity ratio on a mortgage valued at $1,000,000 with a loan of $750,000?

    A. 25%
    B. 50%
    C. 65%
    D. 75%

45. Who controls flood insurance?

    A. FEMA
    B. EPA
    C. CERCLA
    D. FHA

46. What is a detailed building plan that is needed before starting construction?

    A. Building design
    B. Execution plan
    C. Blueprint
    D. Authorized plan

47. What type of house insulation was banned due to the release of formaldehyde fumes?

    A. Foam boards
    B. Loose fill
    C. Vapor barriers
    D. UFFI

48. What is the term used to describe a scenario where an agent represents both the buyer and the seller?

    A. Single agency
    B. Dual agency
    C. Multi agency
    D. Representing both agency

49. Which formal agreement gives an agent the sole right to sell a property?

    A. Purchase agreement
    B. Floating rate
    C. Exclusive Right-to-Sell Agreement
    D. Bridge loan

50. A tenant is legally allowed to remove equipment previously installed to facilitate business operations before the expiry of a lease. Why is this the case?

    A. The equipment is considered trade fixtures
    B. The equipment belongs to the lease holder
    C. The lessor does not want it
    D. It was part of the lease agreement

51. What type of easement attaches rights to an individual rather than the property?

    A. Easement appurtenant
    B. Easement in gross
    C. Prescriptive easement
    D. All of the above

52. What is the name given to the lowest section of the roof that extends into the sidewalls?

    A. Board
    B. Eaves
    C. Joists
    D. Beams

53. Which two parties are responsible for determining the commission earned by the broker?

    A. Seller and agent
    B. Seller and broker
    C. Buyer and agent
    D. Buyer and seller

54. Why must a lawsuit be filed within a specific time after an occurrence?

    A. To prevent the criminal from getting away
    B. Lis pendens
    C. Credibility
    D. Statute of limitations

55. Chris borrows money to purchase a new home and gives the mortgage to the lender as security. What term can be used to refer to Chris?

    A. Mortgagor
    B. Mortgagee
    C. Broker
    D. Buyer

56. What type of lease does a tenant have when he is paying a percentage of gross sales in addition to the base rent?

    A. Proprietary lease
    B. Net lease
    C. Percentage lease
    D. Gross lease

Practice Test 1 – National Portion

57. Why was the Civil Rights Act of 1866 significant in real estate?

- A. It protected against racial discrimination
- B. It protected interests of women
- C. It protected children's rights
- D. It protected against ageism

58. Why was the Privacy Act of 1974 significant?

- A. It required agencies to publicize records to the Federal Register
- B. It required privacy of records
- C. It required federal government to operate without transparency
- D. It required credit information to be kept private

59. Why was the Fair Housing Act of 1968 significant?

- A. It prohibited agents from asking prospective buyers about income
- B. It prohibited discrimination when selling, financing, or renting of a property
- C. It created affordable housing for low-income citizens
- D. None of the above

60. Jack is trying to convince Mary to sell her property in her neighborhood because it is changing due to the influx of people of other ethnic backgrounds. What is he doing?

- A. Steering
- B. Discriminating
- C. Blockbusting
- D. Convincing

61. What is the name of an agreement that allows for conditions on a property?

- A. Contract
- B. Deed
- C. Lease
- D. Qualified fee estate

62. What is **redlining**?

- A. Refusal by lending institutions to grant loans based on race
- B. Refusal by lending institutions to grant loans to people with poor credit scores
- C. Refusal of lending institutions to grant loans based on the agency being used for a purchase
- D. Refusal of a lending institution to make a loan because the area is integrated or populated by culturally diverse people

63. What is a form of co-ownership that involves a husband and wife having equal and undivided interest in the property?

- A. Joint tenancy
- B. Tenancy in common
- C. Tenancy by entirety
- D. Tenancy at will

64. What is the act of a property reverting to the state on death of the owner?

- A. Escheat
- B. Encumbrance
- C. Easement
- D. Suing

65. If you have a loan of $150,000 with an 8% interest, how much do you pay in interest every month?

    A. $1,000
    B. $1,200
    C. $5,000
    D. $12,000

66. Based on their contract, a lender declares the entire balance of the loan due immediately due to default by the borrower. How is this possible?

    A. Payday loans
    B. Alternative financing
    C. Acceleration clause
    D. Lines of credit

67. What type of payment plan allows a borrower to make smaller payments in the early years of a mortgage with payments increasing over time?

    A. Blanket mortgage
    B. Graduated mortgage
    C. Anomalous mortgage
    D. Balloon mortgage

68. What kind of mortgage should you apply for if you are buying more than an individual unit or plot?

    A. Graduated mortgage
    B. Blanket mortgage
    C. Balloon mortgage
    D. Adjustable rate mortgage

69. A salesperson is presented with two offers on a listed property. One is above the listing price and another below, which offer should he present to the seller?

    A. Both offers
    B. The one above the listing price
    C. The one below the listing price
    D. Neither

70. What is the name of a transaction where a seller finances the whole sale or part of the sale of a property for the buyer?

    A. Mortgage
    B. Refinancing
    C. Purchase money
    D. Buydown

71. What is an assessment of the value of a property as of a specific date based on objective data?

    A. CMA
    B. Listing price
    C. Tax value
    D. Appraisal

72. Which toxic metallic element is found in old paint and water pipes?

    A. Mercury
    B. Manganese
    C. Cadmium
    D. Lead

73. What is the amount of space used to calculate the lease payments which includes the shared property's common and service areas?

   A. Rentable square footage
   B. Usable square footage
   C. Common areas
   D. Service areas

74. Which chemical compounds commonly used in coolants and refrigeration contribute to the depletion of the ozone?

   A. CFCs
   B. Tetrafluoroethane
   C. Anhydrous ammonia
   D. Greenhouse gases

75. Which of the following does liability insurance protect you from?

   A. House fire
   B. Injury incurred on property
   C. Flood
   D. All of the above

76. What is a deed used for?

   A. To transfer title rights
   B. An official document proving a bank has loaned money
   C. A pro forma statement
   D. A lien

77. What is the measurement used to show the volatility of a market?

   A. Absorption rate
   B. Fluctuation rate
   C. Inflation
   D. Purchase deviation

78. What is the relationship between a broker and their client called?

   A. Fiduciary
   B. Trustee
   C. Seller disclosure
   D. Subagent

79. What is the law of agency?

   A. Commissions that are collected from both parties
   B. A set of laws that apply to a person who acts on behalf of another person
   C. The ability to accept an offer on behalf of the seller
   D. An authorized agency selling another's property

80. A severance is defined as _____.

   A. Real property that is converted into personal property
   B. Anything that is attached to the property naturally or by a person
   C. A person that is acting under a power of attorney
   D. An agreement between a lender and a borrower in which the borrower pledges collateral on a loan

THIS IS THE END OF THE NATIONAL PORTION.

State Portion

1. How are members of the Pennsylvania Real Estate Commission appointed?

   A. By the Governor
   B. By the Senator
   C. By the Senator
   D. None of the above

2. May a licensed real estate agent appeal decisions against them by the Pennsylvania Real Estate Commission?

   A. Yes, always
   B. Yes, but only in the case of a suspension, not a revocation
   C. Yes, but only once
   D. No, never

3. The owner of Acme Apartments directly employed an on-site property manager to collect rent for the apartments. The on-site manager is required to

   A. Have a salesperson's license
   B. Have a broker's license
   C. Have passed two years at college
   D. Have no licensing requirements

4. Who is responsible for brokerage transactions?

   A. The brokerage recordkeeper
   B. The broker of record
   C. The lead broker
   D. Each individual licensed agent is fully responsible for their personal transactions

Practice Test 1 – State Portion

5. At what stage must a real estate licensee give the Consumer Notice to prospective buyers and tenants?

    A. Initial interview
    B. Closing
    C. Negotiations
    D. Offer

6. Which is NOT a requirement to be a licensed real estate broker in Pennsylvania?

    A. Three years' experience as a licensed salesperson
    B. 200 points' experience from real estate transactions
    C. A degree in real estate from an approved institution
    D. 240 hours of approved education

7. Is dual agency illegal in Pennsylvania?

    A. Yes, always
    B. No, as long as both agents' supervising brokers have been informed
    C. No, as long as both parties give written consent
    D. No, as long as designated agency has also been acknowledged

8. According to the Real Estate Licensing and Registration Act, how many hours are required of a salesperson every two years?

    A. 14
    B. 15
    C. 18
    D. 20

Practice Test 1 – State Portion

9. What is the difference between a qualified associate and an unlicensed real estate assistant or secretary?

    A. A qualified associate works for a salesperson instead of a broker or brokerage
    B. A qualified associate is typically paid a percentage of real estate commissions
    C. A qualified associate must be licensed
    D. There is no difference

10. What is the maximum fine the Pennsylvania Real Estate Commission may impose on a licensed agent for misconduct?

    A. 5% of the agent's yearly average commissions going back three years
    B. 1% of the total real or proposed sale price in the transaction where the agent has behaved improperly
    C. $1000
    D. The commission cannot impose fines, it may only suspend or revoke a license, or refer a case to civil court for damages

11. When may a seller's agent NOT present an offer to their client?

    A. When the agent thinks the offer is too low
    B. When the seller has told the agent to disregard offers below a certain amount
    C. When the seller has specified in writing that the agent should disregard offers below a certain amount
    D. Licensed agents must present all offers, even if they know their client will not accept them

12. What is meant by inducement in real estate?

    A. Failing to disclose material fact to convince a potential buyer to purchase a property
    B. Using threat to move a real estate transaction forward
    C. Closing on a property early without informing all relevant parties
    D. Attempting to convince a client under contract to break their contract for the financial benefit of another agent

13. Which of the following about the Pennsylvania Real Estate Commission is incorrect?

    A. Real estate licensees must follow the rules made by the commission
    B. An independent testing company undertakes the examinations of applicants for real estate licensing, instead of commission
    C. The members of the commission are selected by the state Association of REALTORS®
    D. The commission must submit annual reports to legislative committees in the state senate and house of representatives

14. Which of the following can be left out of a written exclusive listing agreement?

    A. Fee received by the broker
    B. Commission received by the salesperson
    C. Time duration of the listing
    D. Comprehensive legal description regarding the property being sold

15. An agent has entered into agency agreements with both the seller and the buyer of a property. Is this legal?

    A. Yes, as long as the agent informs both parties
    B. Yes, no further action is required of the agent
    C. Yes, as long as both the buyer and seller give the agent written consent
    D. No, dual agency is illegal in the state of Pennsylvania

16. Who is in charge of administering the law in Pennsylvania?

    A. The Department of Buildings
    B. The Secretary of State
    C. The Pennsylvania Real Estate Commission
    D. The State Court

Practice Test 1 – State Portion

17. Which of the following statements regarding the Pennsylvania Real Estate Commission are true?

    A. The Commission does not administer the exam
    B. The Commission makes the rules regarding real estate licensing
    C. The Commission submits annual reports to the Senate and House of Representatives
    D. All of the above

18. At least how many members of the Pennsylvania Real Estate Commission must be licensed real estate brokers?

    A. 5
    B. 6
    C. 7
    D. 8

19. Who is subject to disciplinary action by the Pennsylvania Real Estate Commission?

    A. Time-share salesperson
    B. Cemetery salesperson
    C. Campground salesperson
    D. All of the above

20. If a licensee remains inactive for over five years, what can they do to renew their license?

    A. Retake the real estate licensing course
    B. Retake the licensing exam
    C. Write a letter to the Commission
    D. All of the above

Practice Test 1 – State Portion

21. Is it legal to have three separate offices as a cemetery broker?

    A. Yes, if you have separate branch licenses for each branch office
    B. Yes, if only one of the three is in Pennsylvania
    C. Yes, if permission from the Commission is given
    D. No

22. Which of the following is required when applying for a broker's license?

    A. You must be 21 or older
    B. You must have graduated high school
    C. At least 3 years of real estate experience
    D. All of the above

23. Which of the following would result in license suspension or revocation?

    A. Being legally declared mentally incompetent
    B. Helping another person cheat on the licensing examination
    C. Displaying a "For Sale" sign on a property without the owner's written consent
    D. All of the above

24. A special agent, in real estate, is the same as a _____ agent.

    A. Designated
    B. Limited
    C. Dual
    D. Buyer's or Seller's

Practice Test 1 – State Portion

25. When does a real estate salesperson's license expire in Pennsylvania?

    A. May 31 of every even numbered year
    B. June 15th of every second year
    C. December 31st of every second year
    D. Two years after the date of issuance

26. A licensee owns an investment property in downtown Philadelphia. Under what conditions may the salesperson sell the property?

    A. The salesperson must find an agent to represent him/her
    B. The salesperson may advertise the property as "for sale by owner" but must disclose his/her license status in any ads for the property
    C. The salesperson may act as an agent without disclosing his/her position as the property owner
    D. The salesperson must list the property under his/her employing broker

27. Which of the following is exempt from the provisions of the Real Estate Licensing and Registration Act?

    A. Hospitals
    B. Commercial property
    C. Cemeteries
    D. None of the above

28. How was the Real Estate Licensing and Registration Act (RELRA) amended in 2018?

    A. It reduced the required age from 21 to 18
    B. It increased the amount of required education to 75 hours
    C. t reduced the education requirement from Bachelor's degree to high school diploma
    D. Applicants are now required to have lived in PA for at least 6 months

29. In an agreement of sale, which of the following provisions must be included?

    A. Dates for payment and transference
    B. The deadline of getting a loan from mortgage
    C. Language addressing the buyer's ability to secure mortgage financing
    D. Zoning classification for single family housing

30. What is the minimum age to become a real estate salesperson?

    A. 18
    B. 19
    C. 21
    D. 22

THIS IS THE END OF THE STATE PORTION.

Practice Test 1 – Answers

Answer Key – National Portion

1.	A	21.	A	41.	C	61.	D
2.	B	22.	A	42.	B	62.	D
3.	B	23.	B	43.	A	63.	C
4.	A	24.	D	44.	D	64.	A
5.	D	25.	C	45.	A	65.	A
6.	B	26.	C	46.	C	66.	C
7.	C	27.	C	47.	D	67.	B
8.	D	28.	A	48.	B	68.	B
9.	A	29.	D	49.	C	69.	A
10.	B	30.	B	50.	A	70.	C
11.	B	31.	D	51.	B	71.	D
12.	A	32.	A	52.	B	72.	D
13.	A	33.	A	53.	B	73.	A
14.	C	34.	D	54.	D	74.	A
15.	D	35.	A	55.	A	75.	D
16.	A	36.	A	56.	C	76.	A
17.	B	37.	D	57.	A	77.	A
18.	C	38.	B	58.	A	78.	A
19.	C	39.	B	59.	B	79.	B
20.	D	40.	D	60.	C	80.	A

1. **A) A loan that has a predetermined repayment interest rate**

   Commonly compared to floating rate, which is a loan that uses external factors as a benchmark for interest rates and is usually fluctuating based on the external market.

2. **B) Civil Rights Act of 1866**

   This act declares all citizens equal and under the protection of the law. The law emphasized protecting all citizens of African descent during the Civil War.

3. **B) Promissory note**

   This is a financial document by the issuer to the payee that contains a promise to make payment for a definite sum of money. It is usually valid for payment either on demand or on a specified date. It usually contains information regarding the principal amount, interest rate, date and place of issuance, maturity date and signature of the parties involved.

4. **A) Refinancing**

   This is the process of replacing an existing mortgage with another that offers more favorable terms to the borrower. Refinancing enables a borrower to negotiate for lower monthly payments, lower interest rates and renegotiate the loan payment term.

Practice Test 1 – Answers

5. **D) All of the above**

   An appurtenance is real property fixed to the land that is passed along with the sale of a property.

6. **B) Certificate of deposit**

   This is a product offered by banks and credit facilities to customers enabling them to deposit a lump sum amount for a predetermined period with an agreed upon interest rate premium. Doing some research on the certificate of deposit terms offered by the different available facilities is important to yield better returns.

7. **C) $250,000**

   $225,000 / (1 - 0.1) = $250,000

8. **D) Annual percentage rate**

   This is the annual rate charged on a loan or investment. It is usually used to express the actual annual cost of funds over the lifespan of a loan or cash investment. As loan arrangements vary among institutions and the situation surrounding the loan, a standardized APR is set to protect borrowers from unreasonably high interest rates.

9. **A) Public auctions**

   Homes are usually put on auction due to default on a mortgage or property taxes. Buying a house at an auction is risky as it often does not give the buyer a chance to view the interior of the house. When buying a property at an auction, it is necessary to run background research on the property.

10. **B) Pre-qualification**

    These is the process of reviewing clients' creditworthiness and is usually used as a marketing strategy to obtain new clients. Creditors usually mail a potential borrower outlining maximum limit for loan.

11. **B) Power of attorney**

    This is a legal document that transfers rights to act in place of a principal in the event that they are unable to act for themselves. The terms of the contract usually include what can be managed and where the power of the agent ends.

12. **A) Exclusive listing**

    An exclusive listing is an agreement between a seller and an agent stating that commission on a sale can only be earned when a sale is made within a specified period of time. The timeframe for the sale is usually agreed on by both parties while entering the agreement.

Practice Test 1 – Answers

13. **A) Single agency**

    This is brokerage agreement where a buying agent is assigned the role to represent a buyer and works in single agency capacity as the buyer's agent. This agent is bound by fiduciary duties to the buyer and cannot disclose any confidential information to the other party.

14. **C) Arms-length transaction**

    This is a transaction where both the buyer and the seller are acting in self-interest with an aim of getting the better deal. The discrepancy is usually solved when both parties agree on a middle ground that fulfills the interests of both the buyer and the seller.

15. **D) Adjustment date**

    This is the changing of a date where calculations on items such as property taxes, rent and damage deposits are done.

16. **A) Assumable mortgage**

    This is a mortgage arrangement that allows the seller to transfer the terms and conditions of a mortgage to a buyer. In this case, a buyer absorbs the seller's remaining debt instead of taking out a new mortgage.

17. **B) Call option**

    This is a contract signed by both the buyer and the seller giving one party the right to sell and the other the right to buy a property on a future date. The price of the property is usually included in the contract and remains the same regardless of inflation or market shifts.

18. **C) A specified expiration date**

    An exclusive listing contract is an agreement where a real estate agent receives commission within a specified amount of time. The agent receives commission no matter how the buyer is found.

19. **C) Reciprocity**

    Real estate license reciprocity allows agents to obtain a real estate license in another state by taking the reciprocal state's exam.

20. **D) Privacy**

    The 6 fiduciary duties of a real estate agent are: **O**bedience, **L**oyalty, **D**isclosure, **C**onfidentiality, **A**ccountability, and **R**easonable care / diligence (OLDCAR)

Practice Test 1 – Answers

21. **A) Conditions that must be met by both the buyer and the seller before closing**

    They are set in place to protect the parties involved in the contract. A breach in the contingencies results in the immediate termination of the contract.

22. **A) Any individual whose name appears on the loan document**

    This is often someone whose credit score was taken into consideration when determining whether or not a loan can be extended. A co-borrower can be beneficial for a borrower that is unable to get favorable interest rates.

23. **B) Construction loan**

    This is a short-term loan that is usually taken to finance the construction of a home or real estate property. It is usually taken to provide cash flow before larger funding is approved.

24. **D) Final walkthrough**

    This is a visit done to the property by the buyer after all financing has been secured. A buyer is required to visit the premise and establish whether all the things that were discussed in the contract have been met prior to closing the deal.

25. **C) Fixed mortgage rate**

    This is a mortgage loan whose interest rate remains the same throughout the longevity of the loan.

26. **C) Loan to value ratio**

    This is defined as the percentage of the home's value owned by the borrower after making a down payment. It is calculated by taking the mortgage loan amount and dividing it by the appraisal value of the property being bought. The higher the loan to value ratio, the less likely lenders are to agree to loans.

27. **C) 20%**

    ($1,000 * 12) / $60,000 = 0.2

28. **A) Vicarious liability**

    This is a secondary form of liability where a superior is held accountable for the actions of his subordinates. In the real estate sector, vicarious liability arises when an agent hired by either the buyer or seller acts inappropriately. In this case, the client is held accountable for the misconduct of his agent.

Practice Test 1 – Answers

29. **D) Agency disclosure statement**

    This is a statement signed by both the seller and buyer prior to the real estate transaction. Its role is to disclose the role of the agent in the transaction. An agent can either be a broker for either the buyer or the seller, a dual agent or a sub agent. In order to enforce disclosure laws, some states have a disclosure form written into law.

30. **B) Price fixing**

    This is a situation that arises where a number of real estate agencies that dominate the market agree on a set commission. Brokers are required by law to set their individual commissions where consideration to the market going rate is allowed. Choosing to agree on a set standard commission could result in the suspension of a broker's license. These laws were set in place to protect the buyers and sellers in the market.

31. **D) IRS**

    The IRS uses the general rule that an individual can be classified as an independent contractor if the payer has the right to control the result of work and not how it will be done.

32. **A) Freehold**

    Freehold title is a title given to a freehold property where the owner owns the unit and the land on which the establishment has been developed and anything that is erected on the land.

33. **A) $0**

    According to the Taxpayer Relief Act of 1997, a married couple is eligible for exemption from capital gain tax on profits of up to $500,000. This can only be claimed provided the property is the primary home of the selling couple meaning they have been living there for at least 2 years. Therefore, Mr. and Mrs. Smith do not owe anything in capital gain tax.

34. **D) Suspended**

    He can choose to wait for the suspension to be lifted or look for another broker. A license can be suspended due to violation of insurance laws, providing materially misleading information and fraudulent practices. A revoked can only be reinstated after one year with undeniable evidence of trustworthiness and ability to uphold the law.

35. **A) Umbrella policy**

    An umbrella insurance policy is an excess liability policy that is often used as a fail-safe for assets and savings. It is mostly used by people that are at risk of being sued. Contrary to popular belief, an umbrella policy does not cover additional risk area but acts as an addition to an already existing insurance.

Practice Test 1 – Answers

36. **A) Comparative Market Analysis**

Comparative Market Analysis is never used in valuation as it is based on the market value of similar properties whereas no two real properties are alike.

37. **D) Voidable Contract**

A voidable contract is a formal agreement between parties that can be rendered obsolete due to legal factors. Some of the factors that can result in a voidable contract being rejected are fraud, undisclosed facts and a breach of the contract. A voidable contract is always considered legal unless rendered unenforceable.

38. **B) Disclosure**

Fiduciary duties arise when an agency operates on behalf of a client. In this case the agent is legally mandated to act in the best interest of the client. When an agent fails to disclose facts that may influence the final decision of the client, he is in violation of the disclosure clause.

39. **B) Joint tenancy**

A joint tenancy is an arrangement where two or more parties agree to co-own a property with equal rights and obligations. Upon death of a partner, the property remains solely in the ownership of the surviving partner. A joint tenancy has to be entered at the same time through a deed. Joint tenancy has the advantage of avoiding legal battles after the demise of a partner but can be hard to settle in the event of a divorced couple.

40. **D) Proprietary lease**

A proprietary lease is a is an agreement that allows a shareholder in a housing corporation to live in a unit equaling their stakes in the corporation. A shareholder does not buy the property but shares in the corporation. In this case, the shares act as collateral on the lease.

41. **C) Void**

This means to be obsolete and have no enforceable terms. Parties to a void contract are not bound by its terms making the contract unenforceable.

42. **B) 43,560**

An acre is a standard unit for measuring land. An acre does not have to be square shaped but contains an equivalent of 43560 square feet.

Practice Test 1 – Answers

43. **A) 100 amps**

    The minimum is 100 amps as anything below that may not be able to sustain the electric needs of a home. Larger homes can have between 150 and 200 amps based on the type of electronic systems installed. Having a proper electrical distribution in the home will also avoid trips.

44. **D) 75%**

    750,000 / 1,000,000 = 0.75

    The debt-to-equity ratio is used to determine whether a buyer can afford a house or to refinance an already owned property.

45. **A) FEMA**

    The Federal Emergency Management Agency focuses on promoting the need to work together to support citizens and fast respondents. Its goal is to ensure citizens build and sustain to prepare for and recover from calamities.

46. **C) Blueprint**

    A blueprint is a reproduction of a technical drawing on a light sensitive sheet that is done using a contact printer. A blueprint is usually required to predetermine the design and pattern that is going to be followed in a construction.

47. **D) UFFI**

    Urea Formaldehyde Foam Insulation was used for house insulation in the 70s due to its high thermal resistance. Testing in the lab showed that the insulation produced fumes that were toxic for humans and the environment leading to its ban in 1982.

48. **B) Dual agency**

    Dual agency is legal in Pennsylvania provided both the buyer and the seller agree to the arrangement after pros and cons of the relationship are laid on the table. Opting to have a dual agent means that the client cannot expect the agent to act in their best interest as he is representing two conflicting interests.

49. **C) Exclusive Right-to-Sell Agreement**

    This is an agreement between a seller and agent granting the agent or firm the exclusive right to market and sell a property.

Practice Test 1 – Answers

50. **A) The equipment is considered trade fixtures**

    Trade fixtures are removable personal property that are installed in a leased space to facilitate business running. For one to be allowed to remove a fixture, it must be essential for the running of the business to not cause damage to the property and be removed before the expiry of the lease.

51. **B) Easement in gross**

    The rights associated by the easement are irrevocable for the person granted. A transfer of the property to another individual through sale or inheritance does not warrant an automatic transfer of the rights to the new owner. This renders the easement of gross void.

52. **B) Eaves**

    An eave is the lower edge of a roof that protrude or hangs over the building's side.

53. **B) Seller and broker**

    The seller and broker are usually responsible for agreeing in the amount of commission that should be paid to the broker

54. **D) Statute of limitations**

    The statute of limitations is a law that sets the maximum period of time parties involved in a rift have to initiate legal proceedings from the day of the occurrence of the event. The time allocated to offences differs according to the nature of the offence.

55. **A) Mortgagor**

    A mortgagor is an individual that borrows money from a lender in order to purchase a property. The lending is based on the individual's credit score and collateral. A title must be handed to the lender as collateral for the loan.

56. **C) Percentage lease**

    A percentage lease is a type of lease where the tenant pays rent plus a percentage of any revenue earned while doing business on the property. This agreement significantly reduces the rent paid. The parties involved agree on a base point where percentage lease kicks in.

57. **A) It protected against racial discrimination**

    The Civil Rights act of 1866 banned racial discrimination in real estate and housing transactions. People of any race had equal rights as whites to buy, sell, or lease property.

Practice Test 1 – Answers

58. **A) It required agencies to publicize records to the Federal Register**

The Privacy Act of 1974 is an act that established code of fair information maintenance governing the collection, use and maintenance of individuals that is maintained by federal agencies. The act required the agencies to publicize the records in the Federal Register.

59. **B) It prohibited discrimination when selling, financing, or renting of a property**

The 1968 Act prohibited discrimination based on race, religion, national origin, sex, handicap and family status of the sale, financing, and rental of housing.

60. **C) Blockbusting**

This is the act of trying to manipulate tenants to sell or rent their properties at lower rates due to an influx of minority groups in a once segregated neighborhood.

61. **D) Qualified fee estate**

This is an estate agreement that facilitates the grantor to propose a set of conditions. A breach in the condition limitation may result in termination of the agreement. A quality fee estate can also be based on the occurrence of a predetermined event.

62. **D) Refusal of a lending institution to make a loan because the area is integrated or populated by culturally diverse people**

This usually occurs when a lending institution has a map of areas they would not like to initiate credit in. Potential property owners are denied mortgages despite great credit scores due to the location of the property they intend to purchase.

63. **C) Tenancy by entirety**

Only married couples can enter this type of co-ownership where the property is jointly owned as a single entity. It facilitates right of survivorship and can be terminated upon death of spouse or divorce.

64. **A) Escheat**

A property can be reverted to the state if no claimants have come forth to claim the property or the available heir has been deemed legally unfit to be granted ownership. It is revocable once a legal heir claims the property.

65. **A) $1,000**

($150,000 * 0.08) / 12 = $1,000

Practice Test 1 – Answers

66. **C) Acceleration clause**

This is a contract that allows a lender to require full settlement of an outstanding loan due to a breach of predetermined conditions.

67. **B) Graduated mortgage**

This is a fixed price loan that allows the borrower to make smaller payments on the loan in the earlier payment years and continues to increase gradually until the mortgage is paid off. It considers individuals who were otherwise not qualified for the higher rate to qualify.

68. **B) Blanket mortgage**

A blanket mortgage is a mortgage that covers two or more pieces of real estate. The real estate property is held as collateral. Individual properties can be sold without having to retire the mortgage. This insurance is usually taken when purchasing and developing land.

69. **A) Both offers**

The agent is required by fiduciary duties to present both the offers to the client. Choosing to present the higher offer to the client in order to reap higher commission from the sale is a breach of fiduciary duties.

70. **C) Purchase money**

This is a mortgage issued by the seller as part of a real estate transaction. This arrangement is usually reached when the buyer is not eligible for the traditional mortgage. A down payment is usually placed on the property as an order of the financial transaction.

71. **D) Appraisal**

An appraisal is an opinion usually given by a professional on the market value of a property. Properties usually require an appraisal is unique and market value of similar properties may not offer an accurate value of the property.

72. **D) Lead**

Lead is a periodic metal that was used in paint in the 1970s as it accelerated drying, maintained a fresh appearance and resisted moisture. Older plumbing systems used lead lines and water often corroded the material as it was transported to the consumer's taps. Use of lead in paint was discontinued as it was found to cause nervous system damage and stunted growth in children.

73. **A) Rentable square footage**

Rentable square footage is inclusive of the usable square footage and common areas. The price per rentable square foot is usually calculated using a pro-rata calculation based on the size of the space being leased.

Practice Test 1 – Answers

74. **A) CFCs**

    CFCs are nonflammable chemicals that are commonly used in aerosol sprays and industrial cleaning products. Once these chemicals are released into the atmosphere they rise into the stratosphere where ultraviolet rays from the sun break them down. This breakdown releases chlorine atoms that destroy ozone molecules therefore forming ozone holes.

75. **D) All of the above**

    Liability insurance covers everything from house fires, injuries incurred on the property, floods, injured domestic workers, falling trees, and more.

76. **A) To transfer title rights**

    The buyer and seller must both sign a deed to transfer the property's ownership.

77. **A) Absorption rate**

    This is a ration of the number of properties that have been sold against the number of properties that are available for sale within a specified area.

78. **A) Fiduciary**

    Fiduciary is the relationship between client and broker. An agent is the fiduciary of the client.

79. **B) A set of laws that apply to a person who acts on behalf of another person**

    The law of agency is a set of duties that real estate professionals owe to their clients, including disclosures that must be made to the client. These duties are set by each state.

80. **A) Real property that is converted into personal property**

    There are two types of severance, actual severance and constructive severance. An actual severance is when an item is removed from the land and a constructive severance is when an item is detached by intent.

Practice Test 1 – Answers

Answer Key – State Portion

1.	A	21.	A
2.	C	22.	D
3.	D	23.	D
4.	B	24.	B
5.	A	25.	A
6.	C	26.	B
7.	C	27.	C
8.	A	28.	B
9.	D	29.	A
10.	C	30.	A
11.	C		
12.	D		
13.	C		
14.	D		
15.	C		
16.	C		
17.	D		
18.	A		
19.	D		
20.	B		

1. **A) By the Governor**

All members of the Commission are appointed by the governor.

2. **C) Yes, but only once**

Licensed agents may appeal unfavorable outcomes from the Pennsylvania Real Estate Commission, but once the commission has returned a second unfavorable outcome, the agent cannot then appeal the decision a second time.

3. **D) Have no licensing requirements**

Anyone hired by the owner of property directly for the purpose of managing residential property is excluded under the license law (304 (10)).

4. **B) The broker of record**

The broker of record is responsible for all transactions of a brokerage. The brokerage is licensed under the broker of record, and all other brokers, salespersons, or unlicensed employees work under this broker.

Practice Test 1 – Answers

5. **A) Initial interview**

    The Consumer Notice must be provided to a purchaser/tenant at the initial interview, which is defined as the first contact where a substantive discussion about real estate needs occurs.

6. **C) A degree in real estate from an approved institution**

    In order to become a licensed broker in Pennsylvania, an individual must have three years' experience as a licensed salesperson, 240 hours of approved education, and 200 points' experience from real estate transactions. They must also be at least 21 years of age and have a high school diploma or a GED.

7. **C) No, as long as both parties give written consent**

    Dual agency is a situation where an agent represents both buyer and seller in a transaction. This situation is legal in Pennsylvania as long as both parties have been duly informed and have gien written consent.

8. **A) 14**

    14 hours of Commission-approved continuing education are required during each two-year license period.

9. **D) There is no difference**

    A qualified associate is essentially the same as a real estate assistant or secretary in that the associate may answer phones, make appointments, compile and print literature, and direct clients at open houses to a licensed agent. Qualified associates need not be licensed, are generally paid either salary or hourly, and usually work for brokerages.

10. **C) $1000**

    The Pennsylvania Real Estate Commission may fine a licensed agent an amount up to $1000 for violation of proper conduct, alongside suspending or revoking their license.

11. **C) When the seller has specified in writing that the agent should disregard offers below a certain amount**

    Licensed agents have a duty to present all offers to their client, regardless of perceived quality. However, if the client has specified certain conditions for offers in writing, the agent may disregard offers that do not meet those conditions.

Practice Test 1 – Answers

12. **D) Attempting to convince a client under contract to break their contract for the financial benefit of another agent**

    Licensed agents are prohibited from attempting to interfere with any client-agent relationship for the financial benefit of said licensed agent. This constitutes inducement.

13. **C) The members of the commission are selected by the state Association of REALTORS®**

    Members of the real estate commission are appointed by the governor only (202 (a)), not the state Association of REALTORS® or any other civil body.

14. **D) Comprehensive legal description regarding the property being sold**

    A listing contract is not required to specify the complete legal description of the property being sold. Mandatory provisions of exclusive listing contracts are established by real estate commission regulation (35.332).

15. **C) Yes, as long as both the buyer and seller give the agent written consent**

    In Pennsylvania, dual agency is permitted if both parties give their fully informed consent in writing 606.4(A).

16. **C) The Pennsylvania Real Estate Commission**

    The Pennsylvania Real Estate commission has the power and authority to enforce license laws within the state. This includes regulations over continuing education for licensed agents to license renewal.

17. **D) All of the above**

    Exams are administered through third party testing companies, while licensing is done through the Pennsylvania Real Estate Commission. The Commission is also required to submit reports to the state's Senate and House of Representatives.

18. **A) 5**

    Five members of the Pennsylvania Real Estate Commission must be licensed and have at least ten years of experience working in real estate.

19. **D) All of the above**

    The Real Estate Commission grants and renews licenses to persons who bear a good reputation for honesty, trustworthiness, integrity and competence to transact the business of broker, salesperson, cemetery broker, cemetery salesperson, campground membership salesperson, time-share salesperson, builder-owner salesperson or rental listing referral agent, in such a manner as to safeguard the interest of the public.

Practice Test 1 – Answers

20. **B) Retake the licensing exam**

    Licensees must retake the state real estate licensing exam to obtain another license if they have been inactive for over five years. They are not required to retake licensing courses.

21. **A) Yes, if you have separate branch licenses for each branch office**

    Each office must have its own individual license.

22. **D) All of the above**

    To qualify for a real estate broker license, you must be 21 or older, have at least 3 years of experience, and have graduated high school.

23. **D) All of the above**

    Erecting a "For Sale" sign without written consent is a violation of 604 (a)(8), and the issue of honesty and competency are addressed under 604 (a)(20).

24. **B) Limited**

    A limited, or special, agent is a licensed real estate agent employed to represent a client in one specific transaction. This relationship is neither ongoing nor specifically exclusive, nor does it include expanded agency for the agent on behalf of the client, like power of attorney.

25. **A) May 31 of every even numbered year**

    All licenses expire at the end of the license period established by the commission. Salesperson and broker licenses all expire the last day of May in even-numbered years and must be renewed on or before June 1.

26. **B) The salesperson may advertise the property as "for sale by owner" but must disclose his/her license status in any ads for the property.**

    A licensee who sells or leases his or her own real estate must disclose this licensure in advertisements for the property. This requirement does not apply if the property is listed for sale with a real estate company (35.304).

27. **C) Cemeteries**

    As stated in the official document: "Cemetery companies and cemeteries owned or controlled by a bona fide church or religious congregation or fraternal organization or by any association created by a bona fide church or religious organization or by a fraternal organization."

28. **B) It increased the amount of required education to 75 hours**

    It changed the required amount of real estate courses from 60 to 75 hours.

Practice Test 1 – Answers

29. **A) Dates for payment and transference**

    Rules of the commission provide that an agreement of sale must contain the dates for payment and conveyance (35.333).

30. **A) 18**

    To qualify for a real estate salesperson license, you must be 18 or older.

Practice Test 2

Directions:

1. You have a 120-minute time limit for the national portion, and a 60-minute time limit for the state portion.

2. To pass, you must answer at least 60 out of 80 questions correctly on the national portion **AND** at least 23 out of 30 questions on the state portion.

3. Some questions will require mathematics. You may use a calculator.

4. **Phones and pagers are not allowed. Having either will result in automatic dismissal from the exam and nullification of exam scores.**

Tips:

- Answer all questions even if you are unsure.
- Mark any questions you are stuck on and revisit them after you are done. The exam is timed so make sure you finish as many questions as you can.
- After reading the question, try answering it in your head first to avoid getting confused by the choices.
- Read the entire question before looking at the answers.
- Use the process of elimination to filter out choices that don't seem correct to increase your chances of selecting the correct answer.
- Be aware of important keywords like **not, sometimes, always,** and **never**. These words completely alter the ask of the question so it's important to keep track of them.

PLEASE READ THESE INSTRUCTIONS CAREFULLY.

Practice Test 2

Name: _____   Date: _____

NATIONAL PORTION

1. Ⓐ Ⓑ Ⓒ Ⓓ	31. Ⓐ Ⓑ Ⓒ Ⓓ	61. Ⓐ Ⓑ Ⓒ Ⓓ	
2. Ⓐ Ⓑ Ⓒ Ⓓ	32. Ⓐ Ⓑ Ⓒ Ⓓ	62. Ⓐ Ⓑ Ⓒ Ⓓ	
3. Ⓐ Ⓑ Ⓒ Ⓓ	33. Ⓐ Ⓑ Ⓒ Ⓓ	63. Ⓐ Ⓑ Ⓒ Ⓓ	
4. Ⓐ Ⓑ Ⓒ Ⓓ	34. Ⓐ Ⓑ Ⓒ Ⓓ	64. Ⓐ Ⓑ Ⓒ Ⓓ	
5. Ⓐ Ⓑ Ⓒ Ⓓ	35. Ⓐ Ⓑ Ⓒ Ⓓ	65. Ⓐ Ⓑ Ⓒ Ⓓ	
6. Ⓐ Ⓑ Ⓒ Ⓓ	36. Ⓐ Ⓑ Ⓒ Ⓓ	66. Ⓐ Ⓑ Ⓒ Ⓓ	
7. Ⓐ Ⓑ Ⓒ Ⓓ	37. Ⓐ Ⓑ Ⓒ Ⓓ	67. Ⓐ Ⓑ Ⓒ Ⓓ	
8. Ⓐ Ⓑ Ⓒ Ⓓ	38. Ⓐ Ⓑ Ⓒ Ⓓ	68. Ⓐ Ⓑ Ⓒ Ⓓ	
9. Ⓐ Ⓑ Ⓒ Ⓓ	39. Ⓐ Ⓑ Ⓒ Ⓓ	69. Ⓐ Ⓑ Ⓒ Ⓓ	
10. Ⓐ Ⓑ Ⓒ Ⓓ	40. Ⓐ Ⓑ Ⓒ Ⓓ	70. Ⓐ Ⓑ Ⓒ Ⓓ	
11. Ⓐ Ⓑ Ⓒ Ⓓ	41. Ⓐ Ⓑ Ⓒ Ⓓ	71. Ⓐ Ⓑ Ⓒ Ⓓ	
12. Ⓐ Ⓑ Ⓒ Ⓓ	42. Ⓐ Ⓑ Ⓒ Ⓓ	72. Ⓐ Ⓑ Ⓒ Ⓓ	
13. Ⓐ Ⓑ Ⓒ Ⓓ	43. Ⓐ Ⓑ Ⓒ Ⓓ	73. Ⓐ Ⓑ Ⓒ Ⓓ	
14. Ⓐ Ⓑ Ⓒ Ⓓ	44. Ⓐ Ⓑ Ⓒ Ⓓ	74. Ⓐ Ⓑ Ⓒ Ⓓ	
15. Ⓐ Ⓑ Ⓒ Ⓓ	45. Ⓐ Ⓑ Ⓒ Ⓓ	75. Ⓐ Ⓑ Ⓒ Ⓓ	
16. Ⓐ Ⓑ Ⓒ Ⓓ	46. Ⓐ Ⓑ Ⓒ Ⓓ	76. Ⓐ Ⓑ Ⓒ Ⓓ	
17. Ⓐ Ⓑ Ⓒ Ⓓ	47. Ⓐ Ⓑ Ⓒ Ⓓ	77. Ⓐ Ⓑ Ⓒ Ⓓ	
18. Ⓐ Ⓑ Ⓒ Ⓓ	48. Ⓐ Ⓑ Ⓒ Ⓓ	78. Ⓐ Ⓑ Ⓒ Ⓓ	
19. Ⓐ Ⓑ Ⓒ Ⓓ	49. Ⓐ Ⓑ Ⓒ Ⓓ	79. Ⓐ Ⓑ Ⓒ Ⓓ	
20. Ⓐ Ⓑ Ⓒ Ⓓ	50. Ⓐ Ⓑ Ⓒ Ⓓ	80. Ⓐ Ⓑ Ⓒ Ⓓ	
21. Ⓐ Ⓑ Ⓒ Ⓓ	51. Ⓐ Ⓑ Ⓒ Ⓓ		
22. Ⓐ Ⓑ Ⓒ Ⓓ	52. Ⓐ Ⓑ Ⓒ Ⓓ		
23. Ⓐ Ⓑ Ⓒ Ⓓ	53. Ⓐ Ⓑ Ⓒ Ⓓ		
24. Ⓐ Ⓑ Ⓒ Ⓓ	54. Ⓐ Ⓑ Ⓒ Ⓓ		
25. Ⓐ Ⓑ Ⓒ Ⓓ	55. Ⓐ Ⓑ Ⓒ Ⓓ		
26. Ⓐ Ⓑ Ⓒ Ⓓ	56. Ⓐ Ⓑ Ⓒ Ⓓ		
27. Ⓐ Ⓑ Ⓒ Ⓓ	57. Ⓐ Ⓑ Ⓒ Ⓓ		
28. Ⓐ Ⓑ Ⓒ Ⓓ	58. Ⓐ Ⓑ Ⓒ Ⓓ		
29. Ⓐ Ⓑ Ⓒ Ⓓ	59. Ⓐ Ⓑ Ⓒ Ⓓ		
30. Ⓐ Ⓑ Ⓒ Ⓓ	60. Ⓐ Ⓑ Ⓒ Ⓓ		

Practice Test 2

Name: _____   Date: _____

STATE PORTION

1. Ⓐ Ⓑ Ⓒ Ⓓ
2. Ⓐ Ⓑ Ⓒ Ⓓ
3. Ⓐ Ⓑ Ⓒ Ⓓ
4. Ⓐ Ⓑ Ⓒ Ⓓ
5. Ⓐ Ⓑ Ⓒ Ⓓ
6. Ⓐ Ⓑ Ⓒ Ⓓ
7. Ⓐ Ⓑ Ⓒ Ⓓ
8. Ⓐ Ⓑ Ⓒ Ⓓ
9. Ⓐ Ⓑ Ⓒ Ⓓ
10. Ⓐ Ⓑ Ⓒ Ⓓ
11. Ⓐ Ⓑ Ⓒ Ⓓ
12. Ⓐ Ⓑ Ⓒ Ⓓ
13. Ⓐ Ⓑ Ⓒ Ⓓ
14. Ⓐ Ⓑ Ⓒ Ⓓ
15. Ⓐ Ⓑ Ⓒ Ⓓ
16. Ⓐ Ⓑ Ⓒ Ⓓ
17. Ⓐ Ⓑ Ⓒ Ⓓ
18. Ⓐ Ⓑ Ⓒ Ⓓ
19. Ⓐ Ⓑ Ⓒ Ⓓ
20. Ⓐ Ⓑ Ⓒ Ⓓ
21. Ⓐ Ⓑ Ⓒ Ⓓ
22. Ⓐ Ⓑ Ⓒ Ⓓ
23. Ⓐ Ⓑ Ⓒ Ⓓ
24. Ⓐ Ⓑ Ⓒ Ⓓ
25. Ⓐ Ⓑ Ⓒ Ⓓ
26. Ⓐ Ⓑ Ⓒ Ⓓ
27. Ⓐ Ⓑ Ⓒ Ⓓ
28. Ⓐ Ⓑ Ⓒ Ⓓ
29. Ⓐ Ⓑ Ⓒ Ⓓ
30. Ⓐ Ⓑ Ⓒ Ⓓ

Unauthorized copying or reuse of this page is illegal.

National Portion

1. What is the process of attempting to recover a loan from a borrower that has stopped making payments?

    A. Concession
    B. Final walk through
    C. Foreclosure
    D. Private mortgage insurance

2. What fibrous material causes cancer when released into the air?

    A. Asbestos
    B. Cotton
    C. Textiles
    D. Trunks

3. What are the vertical beams that frame the house?

    A. Frames
    B. Joists
    C. Shingles
    D. Studs

4. What is a reason a broker may be suspended or have their license revoked?

    A. Misrepresentation
    B. Failure to retain clients
    C. Failure to sell property within specified timeframe
    D. None of the above

5. A property manager makes routine rounds to repair air conditioning vents. What is the term used to refer to this?

    A. Aesthetic maintenance
    B. Avoiding depreciation
    C. Preventive maintenance
    D. Proration

6. What is another term that can be used to refer to the lender?

    A. Seller
    B. Mortgagee
    C. Mortgagor
    D. Loanee

7. If a seller nets $150,000 from the sale of her home, and the commission is 4%, how much did the home sell for?

    A. $144,000
    B. $148,500
    C. $156,000
    D. $156,250

8. What is the name given to the restriction of land usage by the local authorities?

    A. Building codes
    B. Denial
    C. Land zoning
    D. Property tax

9. What is the lender required to do once it is a borrower is unable to clear a mortgage?

   A. Threaten borrower
   B. Sell property without court order
   C. Initiate judicial foreclosure
   D. Evict the borrower

10. Which association represents title insurance?

    A. American Land Title Association
    B. CERCLA
    C. Fair Housing Act
    D. FEMA

11. Which law was passed to regulate credit bureaus?

    A. Annuity law
    B. Consumer credit law
    C. Fair Credit Reporting Act
    D. Truth in Lending Act

12. What is the legal right granted to exit a property?

    A. Easement
    B. Escheat
    C. Right of egress
    D. Right of ingress

13. What is the name given to non-monetary investment?

    A. Sweat equity
    B. Investment
    C. Capital
    D. Maintenance

14. What type of arrangement allows a borrower to negotiate a lower interest rate?

    A. Buydown
    B. Mortgage
    C. Purchase money
    D. Purchase price

15. What is a title without any lien?

    A. Clear title
    B. Deed
    C. Freehold
    D. Regular title

16. What is the name given to the breakdown of an individual's credit history?

    A. Credit assessment
    B. Credit report
    C. Financial record
    D. Repayment report

17. What is another term used to describe ownership?

    A. Credit
    B. Equity
    C. Liability
    D. Shares

18. What is the notice filed against a borrower on missing the repayment deadline?

    A. Notice of cessation
    B. Notice to cure
    C. Notice of default
    D. Notice of intention

19. What is the name given to describe the period a lender must keep a loan offer open to the borrower?

    A. Due diligence period
    B. Loan repayment period
    C. Lock-in period
    D. Target hold period

20. Which of the following is a lease break?

    A. When a tenant breaks a rent prior to the date of expiry without a legal reason.
    B. When a tenant terminates a contract once the lease has expired
    C. When a tenant breaks a lease with the agreement of the landlord
    D. When a landlord allows a tenant to sublease his residence

21. What is the term used to refer to a situation where the amount of funds required to meet an obligation are **not** available?

    A. Buydown
    B. Debt to income ratio
    C. Escrow
    D. Shortfall

22. What is the term used to describe a situation where taxes are reduced or completely scrapped to increase buyers in the market?

    A. Tax abatement
    B. Tax exemption
    C. Tax evasion
    D. Duty free

23. A property originally assessed at $500,000 appreciated at 4% the first year and then 5% the year after. What is its current value?

    A. $525,000
    B. $545,000
    C. $546,000
    D. None of the above

24. Which entity performs the percolation test?

    A. Department of State
    B. Building Inspector
    C. Homeowners Association
    D. Department of Health

25. If a property is taxed at 25% with a tax levy of $92,000, what is its assessed value?

    A. $65,000
    B. $115,000
    C. $122,666
    D. $368,000

26. What is the name given to a brief summary of the history of a title?

    A. Abstract of title
    B. Chain of title
    C. Deed chain
    D. History of deed

27. What material is used in construction to cover joints where two or more types of materials meet?

    A. Flashing
    B. Metal
    C. Wood
    D. Joint

28. What is the lowest section of the roof that overhangs beyond the sidewalls of the building?

    A. Eaves
    B. Joists
    C. Stud
    D. Shingles

29. Which real estate metric is found by dividing cash flow by the deposit and settlement costs?

    A. Cash out
    B. Cash on cash return
    C. Lock in period
    D. Loan to value ratio

30. Which board committee is responsible for maintaining the aesthetic view of a town?

    A. Architectural Review Board
    B. Federal government
    C. Municipality
    D. HOA

31. What type of lease is taken on a loft?

    A. Net lease
    B. Gross lease
    C. Percentage lease
    D. Proprietary lease

32. What clause can prohibit having loud parties?

    A. House rules
    B. Regulations
    C. Lease terms
    D. Noise permit

33. What is the measurement used to show the volatility of a market?

    A. Fluctuation rate
    B. Absorption rate
    C. Inflation
    D. Purchase deviation

34. What is the mortgage clause that allows a lender the right to demand immediate payment of a mortgage?

    A. Cancellation clause
    B. Acceleration clause
    C. Prepayment Penalty clause
    D. Release clause

35. Which agreement allows a property holder to cross another person's land?

    A. Easement appurtenant
    B. Easement in gross
    C. Prescriptive easement
    D. None of the above

36. Which of the following is insurance taken out as a protection against malfunctions associated with the acquisition of a new home?

    A. Flood insurance
    B. Homeowner's warranty insurance
    C. HO2
    D. Hazard insurance

37. What is it called when someone takes possession of a property without being the actual title holder?

    A. Acceleration clause
    B. Adverse possession
    C. Easement
    D. Escheat

38. What is a non-possessory interest in property or restrictive covenant burdening the title?

    A. Adverse possession
    B. Easement
    C. Encumbrance
    D. Escheat

39. What is the name given to the long beams that span the piers of a foundation offering support to the floor or ceiling?

    A. Eaves
    B. Frames
    C. Joists
    D. Studs

40. What conveys a grantor's interest in real property?

    A. Agreement
    B. Conveyance
    C. Offering the loan
    D. Title

Practice Test 2 – National Portion

41. What prohibits the solicitation of residential property listings?

    A. Commingling
    B. Non-solicitation order
    C. Regulation Z
    D. Termination of tenancy

42. What is exempt from property taxation?

    A. Colleges
    B. Office buildings
    C. Supermarkets
    D. Unoccupied land

43. Which fiduciary duty is violated by commingling?

    A. Accountability
    B. Disclosure
    C. Obedience
    D. Loyalty

44. What gives the government power to appropriate private property?

    A. Right of first refusal
    B. Riparian rights
    C. Eminent domain
    D. None of the above

45. What is the owner of a building prohibited to do regarding the disabled?

    A. Allow the disabled to be tenants
    B. Make the building accessible to the disabled
    C. Ensure they are treated like other tenants
    D. Refuse modifications for handicapped tenants

46. What act prohibits discrimination based on disability?

    A. The Americans with Disabilities Act of 1990
    B. Fair Housing Act
    C. Civil Rights Act of 1866
    D. Civil Right Act of 1964

47. What is the name given to a property tenure that can be terminated at any time?

    A. Tenancy in sufferance
    B. Terminated tenancy
    C. Tenancy in common
    D. Tenancy at will

48. If you have a loan of $350,000 with a 7% interest, how much do you pay in interest every month?

    A. $2,041
    B. $2,260
    C. $27,125
    D. $31,208

49. What law prohibits any type of discrimination on the basis of sex and gender?

    A. Fair Housing Act
    B. Civil Rights Act of 1866
    C. Civil Rights Act Amendment of 1974
    D. Americans with Disabilities Act

50. In 1988, the Civil Rights Act was amended to include?

    A. Married women
    B. Immigrants
    C. Black people
    D. Handicaps and familial status

51. What is the net income of a property valued at $500,000 and a capitalization rate of 14%?

    A. $70,000
    B. $43,000
    C. $840,000
    D. None of the above

52. What is the name of an appointed official who estimates the value of real property for taxing purposes?

    A. Agent
    B. Assessor
    C. Appraiser
    D. Tax official

53. What is the term used to describe a situation where a mortgage balance decreases due to periodic installments that pay down the principal and interest?

    A. Adjustable-rate mortgage
    B. Amortization
    C. Lock-in period
    D. Fixed-rate mortgage

54. What is an annual tax levied on the value of real property?

    A. Capital gains tax
    B. Real estate tax
    C. Progressive tax
    D. Regressive tax

55. What is the name given to a situation where an individual uses borrowed money to purchase a property?

    A. Buydown
    B. Purchase money
    C. Leverage
    D. Shorting

56. Which air conditioning system facilitates both heating and cooling?

    A. Forced air system
    B. Cooling system
    C. Heating system
    D. Thermostat

57. What is the waiting time for a real estate agent to renew a license once it is revoked?

    A. Two months
    B. One year
    C. Five years
    D. It is never reinstated

58. Who manages a co-op?

    A. Board of directors
    B. CEO
    C. Co-op developers
    D. Tenants

59. What is the value estimating process that uses similar available properties to determine the value of land?

    A. Mirror method
    B. Sales comparison method
    C. Allocation method
    D. Abstraction method

60. Who is required to sign a deed in a real estate transaction?

    A. Attorney
    B. Buyer
    C. Grantor
    D. Lender

61. What is a poisonous gas that comes from the breakdown of minerals in soil?

    A. Ammonia
    B. Chlorine
    C. Helium
    D. Radon

62. What are the rights of a person whose property is adjacent to or crossed by a river?

    A. Exclusive rights to sell
    B. Riparian rights
    C. Rights of first refusal
    D. Right of disclosure

63. What law requires full disclosure of all credit terms for consumer loans under the Truth in Lending Act?

    A. Americans with Disabilities Act
    B. Civil Rights Act
    C. Fair Housing Act
    D. Regulation Z

64. What is the name given to granting priority to an individual to buy or lease a property?

    A. Bundle of rights
    B. Exclusive right to sell
    C. Right of first refusal
    D. Right of possession

65. What is the loss of property value caused by economic or functional factors?

    A. Economic obsolescence
    B. Depreciation
    C. Legal obsolescence
    D. Aesthetic obsolescence

66. What kind of agent is a real estate agent?

    A. Special agent
    B. General agent
    C. Dual agent
    D. Subagent

67. What valuing method is Comparative Market Analysis **not** considered as?

    A. Appraisal
    B. Home valuing
    C. Depreciation valuing
    D. Tax returns valuing

68. What is a specific lien claimed by someone who has performed construction / repair / renovation work on the property and has **not** been paid?

    A. Mechanic's lien
    B. Involuntary lien
    C. Mortgage
    D. Judicial lien

69. What is the bottom piece of a frame that provides a nailing surface for the floor and wall system?

    A. Eaves
    B. Joist
    C. Sill plate
    D. Stud

70. What is a broker allowed to purchase for a real estate salesperson?

    A. Phone
    B. Medical insurance cover
    C. Retirement plan
    D. A company vehicle

71. When does a real estate salesperson first provide the agency disclosure form?

    A. When the deal is about to be closed
    B. After closing the deal
    C. First substantial contact
    D. Never

72. What is the definition of steering?

    A. When you knowingly provide inaccurate information
    B. Guiding families with children into an apartment building with other families with children and away from other buildings
    C. Discriminating against people due to socio-economic status
    D. Failing to provide proof of continuing real estate education

Practice Test 2 – National Portion

73. What is the value of a point on a mortgage?

    A. 1% of loan
    B. 5% of the loan
    C. 10% of the loan
    D. 50% of the loan

74. What type of talent are real estate salespeople?

    A. Assistants
    B. Independent contractors
    C. Part time employees
    D. Full time employees

75. What is the term used to describe a building that is separate from the main house?

    A. Supplemental structure
    B. Accessory building
    C. Secondary land
    D. Shed

76. The estate that provides absolute ownership of land is called?

    A. Fee simple estate
    B. Life estate
    C. Conditional fee estate
    D. Legal life estate

77. Which of the following is an example of community property?

    A. Property that is inherited by the husband through marriage
    B. Income that is earned by one spouse during the marriage
    C. Income earned prior to marriage
    D. A gift given to one spouse during the marriage

78. Fixture are considered _____.

    A. Hypothecation
    B. An agreement between the two parties
    C. Items that are removable by the tenant before the expiration date of the lease
    D. Real property

79. The commission that is due to a salesperson is decided by?

    A. Chattels
    B. State Law
    C. Mutual Agreement
    D. Court Decree

80. A real estate broker has become an agent of the seller when ____.

    A. A listing agreement with the seller has been executed
    B. They are responsible for sharing commissions
    C. A broker acts in good faith
    D. They are procuring cause

THIS IS THE END OF THE NATIONAL PORTION.

State Portion

1. A licensed attorney in good standing may _____.

   A. Have education requirements for becoming a licensed broker waived
   B. Work as a licensed broker so long as they submit an application
   C. Work as a licensed real estate salesperson with no restriction
   D. Licensed attorneys gain no special benefits in the field of real estate

2. Which of the following agreements must be in writing in order to be enforceable according to the Pennsylvania Statute of Frauds?

   A. Seven-year lease for an apartment in a multifamily building
   B. Two-year lease for an apartment in a condo
   C. One-month commercial lease negotiated by a broker representing the building owner
   D. Commercial lease for a five-year term

3. If a salesperson owns a duplex investment property, the salesperson

   A. Must disclose his/her licensed status to prospective tenants
   B. Must deposit all rent collected into an escrow
   C. Must list the units for rent under his broker
   D. None of the above

4. Which of the following states does the Pennsylvania Real Estate Commission have a reciprocity agreement with?

   A. Connecticut
   B. Georgia
   C. Ohio
   D. New Jersey

5. Which of the following penalties upon conviction for a first offense are applicable if an individual without a license engages in such activities which requires a real estate license?

    A. Fine not to exceed $500
    B. Civil penalty of $8,000
    C. No fine but imprisonment of 5 years
    D. A fine of $10,000 and mandatory imprisonment of 10 months

6. Which of the following is **not** a member of the Pennsylvania Real Estate Commission?

    A. Commissioner of Professional and Occupational Affairs
    B. Director of the Bureau of Consumer Protection
    C. Secretary of the Commonwealth
    D. Three members representing the public

7. Which of the following is a requirement to apply for a Pennsylvania real estate salesperson's license?

    A. You must be at least 21 years old
    B. You must have at least a Bachelor's degree
    C. You must show proof that you are currently unemployed
    D. You must submit evidence that you have completed the required coursework

8. If a licensee violates requirements regarding Consumer Notice at the initial interview, what are the consequences?

    A. The licensee's broker will have his/her license revoked for failing to supervise the licensee
    B. The consumer must file a written complaint in order for there to be a violation
    C. The licensee may have his/her license revoked or suspended
    D. All agreements made with the consumer are voided

Practice Test 2 – State Portion

9. Which of the following is the Pennsylvania Real Estate Commission's statutory authority?

    A. Determining what subjects are on the PA real estate licensing exam
    B. Approving real estate licensing schools
    C. Waive the continuing education requirement for licensees with emergencies, illnesses, or hardship
    D. All of the above

10. With regard to Pennsylvania state: Which of the following statements correctly corresponds to the event, when a broker is listing a home and asks the seller to complete a property condition disclosure?

    A. An agent should provide the broker with partially filled property condition disclosure to safeguard seller's interest
    B. The seller should be informed that Pennsylvania statute requires him/her to disclose the property conditions
    C. The disclosures are optional, and the seller may refuse to make any disclosures about the condition of the property
    D. The required disclosure only covers a minimal detail of the structural conditions

11. A disciplinary action may be taken by the Pennsylvania Real Estate Commission against a licensee when violation of the following occurs **EXCEPT**

    A. Pennsylvania Human Relations Act
    B. Rules specified by the Pennsylvania Real Estate Commission
    C. Real Estate Licensing and Registration Act
    D. Sherman Antitrust Act

12. How must the broker of record's information be displayed on a salesperson's print ad?

    A. Ads must display the name of the broker of record
    B. Ads must display the name and contact information of the broker of record
    C. Ads must display the name and contact information of the broker of record, and it must be at least the same size as the salesperson's information
    D. There are no requirements to display the broker of record's information

Practice Test 2 – State Portion

13. In practice, what is the main difference between a licensed salesperson and an associate broker?

    A. Associate brokers tend to garner a higher percentage of a commission
    B. Associate brokers do not have to be licensed
    C. Associate brokers may co-own a brokerage
    D. Associate brokers are not primarily engaged in buying and selling real estate

14. Which duty do agents only owe in agency relationships, not to customers in general?

    A. Fiduciary
    B. Honesty
    C. Good faith
    D. Compliance with the law

15. In Pennsylvania, a candidate for a broker's license must

    A. Have cleared the broker's license examination within three years prior to license application
    B. Be a college graduate
    C. Be a citizen of the United States
    D. Have two years of experience in real estate sales

16. As a thank you gift for selling his house, a seller sends a bonus check to a Joe, the agent. Joe worked really hard to close the deal so thanks the seller and cashes the check. Which of the following is true?

    A. Accepting the money is legal since it was voluntarily sent by the seller
    B. Accepting the money is legal only if it is split between the agent and broker
    C. Accepting the money is legal because it was given as a check, not as cash
    D. Accepting the money is a violation of the License and Registration Act

17. By what procedure or body are members of the Pennsylvania Real Estate Commission appointed?

    A. By the state governor
    B. By conducting public voting
    C. By a committee of the State Association of REALTORS®
    D. None of the above

18. What is the number of Pennsylvania Real Estate Commission members required to be licensed real estate brokers at the time of their appointment?

    A. 5
    B. 6
    C. 8
    D. 10

19. Administration of the real estate license law in Pennsylvania is done by:

    A. The State Court
    B. Department of Housing and Urban Development
    C. Department of Buildings
    D. The Pennsylvania Real Estate Commission

20. The Pennsylvania Real Estate Commission has the power to:

    A. Cancel the state exam
    B. Formulate and enforce the rules by which all real estate licensees must abide
    C. Change the examination questions on the state exam
    D. Formulate policies which govern real estate licensees

21. The commission / authorized representative during the course of an inspection, will be permitted to do all of the following **EXCEPT**

    A. To access records of the broker's escrow account, written authorization can be acquired
    B. Inspect office space completely
    C. Interview consumers who are currently conducting business during the inspection
    D. Examine records of real estate transactions

22. By authority, the Pennsylvania Real Estate Commission can perform all of the following duties **EXCEPT**

    A. Recommend the subjects to be tested on license examinations
    B. Issue licenses and registration certificates to persons who comply with provisions established by the license law.
    C. Approve schools conducting study courses for real estate
    D. Due to illness, emergency, or hardship; waive all or part of the continuing education requirement for a salesperson or broker

23. Disciplinary action by the Pennsylvania Real Estate Commission applies to which of the following subject?

    A. Attorney
    B. Banking officers handling real estate transactions
    C. Broker and sellers
    D. Campground membership salesperson

24. The licensee may face disciplinary action if certain topics are not included in exclusive listing agreements. All of the following must be included in the listing agreement **EXCEPT**

    A. The broker protection clause
    B. The specified commission rate or amount
    C. The specific termination date
    D. The asking price

25. To obtain a real estate salesperson's license in Pennsylvania, what requirements must be met?

    A. Citizenship of United States
    B. An associate degree in real estate from an accredited college
    C. To own at least one individual personal property in Pennsylvania
    D. 75 classroom hours of instruction in courses prescribed by the commission must be completed successfully

26. Which action constitutes comingling of funds?

    A. A broker depositing earnest money into their operating funds
    B. A broker withdrawing from their operating account to pay payroll taxes
    C. A seller's broker splitting a commission with the buyer's broker
    D. Depositing client earnest money into a broker's custodial account

27. An investigation by the Pennsylvania Real Estate Commission of a licensee can be conducted based on the following grounds **EXCEPT**

    A. A complaint by a consumer
    B. Its own initiative
    C. A random selection of licensees currently active
    D. A motion from the members of the commission

28. For selling a particular listing within the next 30 days, a listing broker offers a $500 bonus to that salesperson. Which of the following is correct?

    A. The seller must approve of the bonus
    B. The seller must approve of the bonus
    C. The broker may only pay the bonus to a salesperson who is employed by the listing broker
    D. The seller must directly pay the bonus for selling property

Practice Test 2 – State Portion

29. Which of the following would cause a disciplinary action against a broker?

  A. Permission to hold open houses for the public before completion training program by a newly licensed salesperson
  B. Paying a bonus directly to a licensed salesperson employed by another licensed broker
  C. Keeping a salesperson employed if found guilty of making a misrepresentation even if the broker had no prior knowledge of the misrepresentation
  D. Requiring associate brokers to agree to non-compete clauses in their employment contracts

30. When are statements of estimated cost and return provided to the parties to a transaction by the broker involved in the transaction?

  A. Before an agreement of sale is executed by the parties
  B. Two business days prior to settlement of the transaction
  C. Within five days of the buyer's loan application
  D. Within seven days of the buyer's loan application

THIS IS THE END OF THE STATE PORTION.

Practice Test 2 – Answers

Answer Key – National Portion

1.	C	21.	D	41.	B	61.	D
2.	A	22.	A	42.	A	62.	B
3.	D	23.	C	43.	A	63.	D
4.	A	24.	D	44.	C	64.	C
5.	C	25.	D	45.	D	65.	A
6.	B	26.	A	46.	A	66.	A
7.	D	27.	A	47.	D	67.	A
8.	C	28.	A	48.	A	68.	A
9.	C	29.	B	49.	C	69.	C
10.	A	30.	A	50.	D	70.	A
11.	C	31.	B	51.	A	71.	C
12.	C	32.	A	52.	B	72.	B
13.	A	33.	B	53.	B	73.	A
14.	A	34.	B	54.	B	74.	B
15.	A	35.	A	55.	C	75.	B
16.	B	36.	B	56.	A	76.	A
17.	B	37.	B	57.	B	77.	B
18.	C	38.	C	58.	A	78.	D
19.	C	39.	C	59.	D	79.	C
20.	A	40.	B	60.	C	80.	A

1. **C) Foreclosure**

   This is the legal process where a lender seeks to recover the balance of a loan by selling the property held as collateral. Foreclosure usually occurs after a lender has legally obtained a termination of the borrower's right of redemption.

2. **A) Asbestos**

   Asbestos is a naturally occurring mineral and its insulation qualities make it popular in making fireproof materials. When products containing asbestos are disturbed, they release tiny fibers in the air that when inhaled over a long period of time can be detrimental as they accumulate in the lung causing scarring and inflammation. Continued exposure affects cells resulting in a rare cancer known as mesothelioma.

3. **D) Studs**

   These are vertical beams that are used during construction to frame the house. They are used to form or position walls in a building. Previously, studs made of timber dominated the construction industry but modern construction styles have embraced the use of steel.

Practice Test 2 – Answers

4. **A) Misrepresentation**

Misrepresentation occurs when a broker misstates information of property. It is a false statement that may affect a person's decision to enter into a contract. Three types of misrepresentation are fraudulent misrepresentation, negligent misrepresentation and innocent misrepresentation.

5. **C) Preventive maintenance**

In order to maintain tenants and an acceptable return on an investment, routine checks and repairs have to be done. These are done to safeguard against failing which may incur losses to the property manager that arise due to cost of replacement.

6. **B) Mortgagee**

A mortgagee is an entity that lends money for the purpose of buying a real estate property. As a precaution, the mortgagee establishes prior interest in the property and maintains the title as collateral.

7. **D) $156,250**

$150,000 / (1 - 0.04) = $156,250

8. **C) Land zoning**

This refers to the restriction of physical development and the use of certain parcels of land. It is done with regard to zoning laws and purposes to protect wildlife and natural resources. It is also used to restrict the number of domestic animals that can be accommodated on a property.

9. **C) Initiate judicial foreclosure**

Judicial foreclosure are court proceedings that allow the lender to seize the property that was held as collateral for sale. This is done in order to regain the principal amount. This can only be done once it has been established that a defaulting borrower is unable to continue making payments.

10. **A) American Land Title Association**

This is a trade association that is aimed at trying to improve oversight by representing title insurance.

Practice Test 2 – Answers

11. **C) Fair Credit Reporting Act**

    Credit reporting is the process of collecting and analyzing consumers credit information by credit bureaus. This information is sold to lending facilities in order to help them determine whether or not a borrower is eligible for a loan. This act was passed to highlight consumer rights when it comes to credit information.

12. **C) Right of egress**

    This is the legal right granted to homeowners as they allow access to property. These rights are usually obtained through an easement and apply regardless of the property type.

13. **A) Sweat equity**

    This is the non-monetary equity that owners contribute into the business or property. In this case, sweat equity is the amount of effort an owner puts into a property in order to increase its value.

14. **A) Buydown**

    This is a mortgage-financing technique that allows a borrower to negotiate lower monthly payment rates. It usually involves the seller making payments to the lending institution to reduce monthly payment rate of the buyer. As a result, the purchase price goes up.

15. **A) Clear title**

    A clear title is a title that has no liens or levies from creditors and other involved parties. A clear title is used to ensure there is no question of ownership. It shows that there are no outstanding financial responsibilities attached to the property and the owner is legally capable of selling the property.

16. **B) Credit report**

    A credit report is a detailed breakdown of an individual's credit history and is usually carried out by credit bureaus. They use financial information attached to an individual like their bill payment to establish a unique report. This information is usually used by lenders while considering a loan applicant.

17. **B) Equity**

    Equity is another term for ownership. In home investments, equity means the amount of principal that has been paid off. The higher the equity the easier it is to refinance a property.

Practice Test 2 – Answers

18. **C) Notice of default**

    This is a public notice filed in court regarding a borrower's default on a loan. It is usually to notify the borrower that there has been a breach in the contractual limit that had been predetermined in the loan. A grace period is included for negotiation before further action is considered.

19. **C) Lock-in period**

    This is the period usually 30 to 60 days within which a lender is required to keep a loan offer open. This gives the borrower enough time to prepare for closing while the lender is processing the loan. A lock in period protects the borrower from losses incurred throughout the repayment of the loan caused by rising interest rates during processing of the loan.

20. **A) When a tenant breaks a rent prior to the date of expiry without a legal reason.**

    As a lease is a contract, breaking a lease without a valid reason may result in being sued by the landlord. To avoid legal action, the individual breaking the lease must prove beyond reasonable doubt that the break was caused by a situation completely out of their hands.

21. **D) Shortfall**

    Shortfall is a term used to describe a situation where a financial obligation exceeds the required amount of cash available. A shortfall may be a temporary and current situation or a prolonged one. The latter represents mismanagement of funds and warrants a deeper look into spending habits and change has to be implemented.

22. **A) Tax abatement**

    Tax abatement is a strategy used by the government to increase investments in specific areas. In the real estate sector, tax abatement occurs when taxes on properties are significantly reduced or completely eliminated. It is usually done to encourage investors to buy property in areas that have recorded long term low demand.

23. **C) $546,000**

    $500,000 * 1.04 * 1.05 = $546,000

24. **D) Department of Health**

25. **D) $368,000**

    $92,000 / 0.25 = $368,000

Practice Test 2 – Answers

26. **A) Abstract of title**

    This is a summarized history of all title transfers and legal actions that have been connected with a certain property. It is beneficial in preventing home buyers from getting tangled in legal issues that are attached to a property. This is because any loss made because of a court ruling on a property once a buyer has purchased will be incurred by the new tenant.

27. **A) Flashing**

    This is a material used to cover joints where two or more types of material join. This usually happens to prevent water leakage through the joint. It also provides a drainage between two joints.

28. **A) Eaves**

    This is a part of the roof that projects over the wall beyond the edge of the roof. It is usually set in place to channel water away from the roof.

29. **B) Cash on cash return**

    Cash on cash return that a proven metric used to calculate future cash returns on a cash investment. This metric is only true for a cash investment and does not take into account loan investments.

30. **A) Architectural Review Board**

    The Architectural Review Board is given the responsibility of upholding the visual integrity of a town. It is responsible for reviewing all exterior designs of all residential and commercial structures in a town. All new structures and structures that are up for alteration are required to provide a blueprint of the exterior design for printing. They are also charged with ensuring commercial signs conform to the towns design.

31. **B) Gross lease**

    A gross lease is a lease where a flat rent fee is paid. It includes rent and other utility fees such as taxes and insurance. A landlord is obligated to calculate a rate based on history or research. A negotiation between the tenant and landlord can also be reached on the services the tenant wants to be included in the lease.

32. **A) House rules**

    These are rules that are given to tenants of a coop or condo on the beginning of the contract regarding behavior within the complex. They are put in place to ensure a comfortable living space for all occupants. Failure to adhere to the rules may result in eviction.

Practice Test 2 – Answers

33. **B) Absorption rate**

    This is a ration of the number of properties that have been sold against the number of properties that are available for sale within a specified area.

34. **B) Acceleration clause**

    This is a provision in a mortgage that allows the lender the right to demand the immediate settlement on a mortgage under certain predetermined conditions such as a borrower defaulting on a loan.

35. **A) Easement appurtenant**

    Easement appurtenant is an agreement that is transferable with ownership rights of a property. When a property is transferred through sale or inheritance, all rights and privileges attached to the land are automatically transferred to the new owner.

36. **B) Homeowner's warranty insurance**

    Homeowner's warranty insurance insures the homeowner from the builder's faults for a specified warranty period

37. **B) Adverse possession**

    This is a legal principle that allows a person who has been living on a specific land for a long period of time to take possession of the land without permission of the owner. The individual does not have to have a title to the land to acquire it. The title holder is capable of claiming his land by choosing to eject the squatter.

38. **C) Encumbrance**

    This is a limitation against a real estate property. It restricts the owner from transferring ownership of the title. It also prevents an owner from depreciating the value of the property.

39. **C) Joists**

    These are horizontal structural members used to frame an open space. They are often used in transferring loads to the vertical members of the structure. When used in floors, they provide stiffness in the framing systems.

40. **B) Conveyance**

    A conveyance or sale deed is a legally binding contract that transfers all ownership rights from the seller to the buyer. It usually states the agreed-on price, the date of the transaction and the obligations of the parties involved.

Practice Test 2 – Answers

41. **B) Non-solicitation order**

    This is an order issued to broker and agents to prevent them from soliciting listings in designated areas

42. **A) Colleges**

    Despite the fact that all property is assessed to determine its value, universities, schools, parks, government institutions, religious organizations, and hospitals are exempt from property taxes. Veterans are also eligible from partial exemption from taxes.

43. **A) Accountability**

    Commingling is a contract breach where a fiduciary mixed funds belonging to a client with his own making it impossible to separate them. The accountability clause requires a fiduciary to be able to maintain an accurate report of documents and funds that he/she has been entrusted.

44. **C) Eminent domain**

    This is the government's power to take private land for public use under certain circumstances. It is defined by the Taking Clause of the Fifth Amendment which prohibits the taking of private land without just compensation. It emphasizes that the government can only take land for public use and offer just compensation on the land.

45. **D) Refuse modifications for handicapped tenants**

    Refuse to allow tenants to make reasonable structural modifications to a unit at the tenant's expense to allow the handicapped tenant full enjoyment of the property (Fair Housing Act). In accordance with the Fair Housing Act which is against discrimination in housing, multifamily buildings are expected to ensure accessibility for people using wheelchairs

46. **A) The Americans with Disabilities Act of 1990**

    This act was enacted to ensure disabled people are not discriminated against and have equal rights regarding access to employment and commercial facilities.

47. **D) Tenancy at will**

    This is a tenancy that is not bound by a lease and does not have an expiry or duration of tenancy. A predetermined payment plan is adhered and a tenant is flexible to terminate the tenancy without legal proceedings. It is a beneficial plan for landlords and tenants that seek flexibility.

48. **A) $2,041**

    ($350,000 * 0.07) / 12 = $2,041

Practice Test 2 – Answers

49. **C) Civil Rights Act Amendment of 1974**

    The Civil Rights act amendment of 1974 banned discrimination based on sex and credit in a congress proceeding. Women being offered maternity leave on the assumption that they were unable to work was rendered illegal and sexist teaching methods were discredited.

50. **D) Handicaps and familial status**

    The act protects people with disabilities and families with children. Pregnant women were also protected from illegal discrimination.

51. **A) $70,000**

    $500,000 * 0.14 = $70,000

52. **B) Assessor**

    An assessor is a government official that is engaged to determine the value of a property. The information gathered by an assessor is used to calculate future property taxes. Assessors maintain annual assessments at a uniform percentage of market value.

53. **B) Amortization**

    This is the scheduling of monthly mortgage payments showing breakdown of payment. When paying a mortgage loan for a property, the initial payments are put towards paying off the interest and less is allocated to the principal amount. As a borrower makes more payments, more is allocated to the principal and less to the interest.

54. **B) Real estate tax**

    This is an ad valorem tax on the value of a property. It is levied annually on real estate by the government authority.

55. **C) Leverage**

    This refers to money that has been borrowed to finance an investment property. The leverage concept works best when rent and property values are on the rise. Monthly mortgage payments for the rental property become constant which results in a rise in profits

56. **A) Forced air system**

    A forced air system refers to any HVAC system that makes use of air ducts and vents to release temperature-controlled air into the building. A forced air system released filtered and dehumidified cold air into buildings and runs at an affordable price. A central air system on the other hand uses vents in the forced air system to provide cool and conditioned air.

Practice Test 2 – Answers

57. **B) One year**

An individual is required to wait for an entire year after which the agent is required to prove with evidence that he/she is capable of being trustworthy and upholding the law with regard to the real estate sector.

58. **A) Board of directors**

A co-op is an alternative method to traditional housing. A board of directors is elected by the shareholders to run the corporation. They are responsible for vetting and doing background checks on potential new shareholders in the corporation. They are also responsible for upholding the values and regulations of the co-op and terminating tenancy of individuals found to be acting contrary to the rules.

59. **D) Abstraction method**

This is a method of estimating the value of a piece of land that is based on the going price of similar parcels of land within the area.

60. **C) Grantor**

This is the party that transfers ownership of property to buyer through a legal document known as a deed. The grantor is required to sign the deed admitting the transfer of ownership before closing. The deed is then filed at the county jurisdiction for public record.

61. **D) Radon**

Radon is a radioactive cancer-causing gas that comes from the natural breakdown of uranium in soil. The gas penetrates its way into houses from cracks and holes in the foundation. Testing for radon gas is mandatory during purchasing of a home in order to fix the problem by lowering the amount of radon gas available to the acceptable amounts.

62. **B) Riparian rights**

These are rights that arise when an individual owns land near a moving watercourse. These rights include swimming and irrigation. The rights only attach when there's a water on one side of the land. An individual is allowed to benefit from the water body without contaminating or altering the flow of the waterbody.

63. **D) Regulation Z**

It requires lenders to make comprehensive disclosure statements to borrowers for consumer loans. It is aimed at protecting consumers from misleading lending practices. Lenders are required to disclose interest rates, finance charges, explain terms used and respond to all complaints launched by the borrower. This law was passed to ensure that borrowers make informed credit choices.

Practice Test 2 – Answers

64. **C) Right of first refusal**

This is the right given to a specific party to purchase or lease a property before it is open to bidding by other potential buyers. The party being offered the privilege is not obligated to buy the property. In the event that the party is not interested in the property, it is opened up to the public.

65. **A) Economic obsolescence**

This is the decrease in the market value of a property due to external factors that cannot be controlled by the property owner i.e. building of an interstate highway close to a prime property. Its value immediately decreases due to the noise pollution.

66. **A) Special agent**

A special agent is an agent whose services are only employed for a specific task. Once the task is completed a special agent no longer has authority to represent the client.

67. **A) Appraisal**

An appraisal in a professional opinion value assessment of a property and is independent of the market values of similar properties based on the fact that all properties are unique and cannot be compared to each other.

68. **A) Mechanic's lien**

This is a security interest in title of property for the benefit of those who supplied materials and offered professional services on the construction and renovation of a property. A mechanic's lien can be taken on both real and personal properties.

69. **C) Sill plate**

This is a horizontal member of a wall where vertical members of the building are attached. It usually lies between the foundation and floor frame.

70. **A) Phone**

This is because salespeople are considered independent contractors and therefore are not eligible for company benefits.

71. **C) First substantial contact**

This refers to the earliest practicable opportunity during a conversation with the consumer. An agency disclosure is to be provided to disclose and explain the nature of the representation in a real estate transaction.

Practice Test 2 – Answers

72. **B) Guiding families with children into an apartment building with other families with children and away from other buildings**

    Steering is an unlawful practice that violates the federal fair housing provisions. It is a practice in which brokers influence the choice of a prospective buyer or tenant.

73. **A) 1% of loan**

    A value point is a fee paid directly to the lender at closing in exchange for a reduced interest rate and can lower a borrower's monthly mortgage payment.

74. **B) Independent contractors**

    Independent contractors are hired to perform a service but are not included in the employee catalogue. Their main goal is to complete the task and the employing broker has no control over the process of yielding results or financial expenses incurred.

75. **B) Accessory building**

    This is a building that is built separately from the main structure in a property. It is usually put to use for a specific purpose such as a shed, workshop or garage.

76. **A) Fee simple estate**

    This provides absolute ownership of the land and allows the owner to do whatever they choose to with the land. This is the highest form of ownership in real estate.

77. **B) Income that is earned by one spouse during the marriage**

    Community property is defined as everything that a married couple owns together. This includes income and property acquired during the duration of the marriage.

78. **D) Real property**

    A fixture is physically property that is permanently attached to real property (on it or under it), that cannot be moved. Examples include ponds, canals, buildings and roads.

79. **C) Mutual Agreement**

    An agreement between a buyer and a seller. It is a binding contract between the two parties and includes any contingencies.

80. **A) A listing agreement with the seller has been executed**

    A listing agreement is a contract between the homeowner and a selling agent. It is a legal agreement that gives the selling agent the right to sell the home.

Practice Test 2 – Answers

Answer Key – State Portion

1.	A	21.	C
2.	D	22.	B
3.	A	23.	D
4.	B	24.	A
5.	A	25.	D
6.	C	26.	A
7.	D	27.	C
8.	C	28.	C
9.	D	29.	B
10.	B	30.	A
11.	D		
12.	C		
13.	A		
14.	A		
15.	A		
16.	D		
17.	A		
18.	A		
19.	D		
20.	B		

1. **A) Have education requirements for becoming a licensed broker waived**

    Attorneys licensed in Pennsylvania may submit a letter of good standing from the Pennsylvania Supreme Court in lieu of completing education requirements in order to become a licensed real estate broker

2. **D) Commercial lease for a five-year term**

    A lease for a term of more than three years must be written in order to be enforceable. In Pennsylvania, leases may be written, oral, or implied. The Statute of Frauds in Pennsylvania applies to leases for more than three years' duration.

3. **A) Must disclose his/her licensed status to prospective tenants**

    A salesperson who is selling or leasing his or her own real estate is required to disclose his or her licensed status to a prospective buyer or lessee before an agreement is entered into. Rents are not deposited into an escrow account. Only the employing broker may compensate a licensed salesperson employed by that broker (35.288).

4. **B) Georgia**

    The commission has a reciprocity agreement with: Arkansas, Georgia, Louisiana, Maryland, Massachusetts, and New York.

Practice Test 2 – Answers

5. **A) Fine not to exceed $500**

Upon conviction for a first offense for practicing real estate without a license, the maximum penalty is a fine not exceeding $500, imprisonment not exceeding three months, or both (303).

6. **C) Secretary of the Commonwealth**

The Pennsylvania Real Estate Commission consists of the Commissioner of Professional and Occupational Affairs, Director of the Bureau of Consumer Protection, three members representing the public, and five other experienced professionals who have had at least ten years working in real estate

7. **D) You must submit evidence that you have completed the required coursework**

Evidence of completion of 75 hours of basic real estate courses within 10 years prior to the exam is required, along with documentation of your past criminal history.

8. **C) The licensee may have his/her license revoked or suspended**

The salesperson's failure to provide the Consumer Notice at the initial interview is a violation of the license law (604(a)(15.1)). Licensees are subject to disciplinary action by the commission including possible suspension or revocation of their licenses.

9. **D) All of the above**

The Commission is the entity in charge of all things licensing (law, education) and has the power to waive a licensee's continuing license requirement if ample evidence is provided that the licensee is unable to fulfill the requirement due to certain circumstances.

10. **B) The seller should be informed that Pennsylvania statute requires him/her to disclose the property conditions**

The licensee should advise the seller about the requirements of the disclosure and ensure the seller's obligation to fulfil the requirements of the statute. The property condition disclosure requirements relate to almost all of the residential transactions and cover a wide spectrum of problems affecting the property.

11. **D) Sherman Antitrust Act**

Antitrust laws are to be enforced by federal and state agencies other than the Pennsylvania Real Estate Commission

Practice Test 2 – Answers

12. **C) Ads must display the name and contact information of the broker of record, and it must be at least the same size as the salesperson's information**

    Real estate print ads by licensed salespersons must include the legal name and contact information of the salesperson as well as the name and contact information of the broker of record. The broker of record's information must be at least as large as the salesperson's in order to make clear that the salesperson is supervised by a broker.

13. **A) Associate brokers tend to garner a higher percentage of a commission**

    Associate brokers are licensed brokers working under a broker of record as a salesperson. In practice, however, associate brokers and salespersons perform similar duties. Due to their higher status and (often) greater experience, associate brokers tend to garner higher percentages of commissions than salespersons.

14. **A) Fiduciary**

    Licensed agents owe all customers, regardless of affiliation, honesty, compliance with the law, and dealings in good faith. Agency relationships include the requirement of fiduciary duty of obedience, loyalty, diligence, care, and accounting.

15. **A) Have cleared the broker's license examination within three years prior to license application**

    The application must be received by the commission within three years of the date of passing the license exam (512 (c)).

16. **D) Accepting the money is a violation of the License and Registration Act**

    The License and Registration Act prohibits accepting a commission or any valuable consideration by a salesperson or associate broker for the performance of any acts specified in this act, from any person, except the licensed real estate broker with whom he is affiliated.

17. **A) By the state governor**

    Each member of the Pennsylvania Real Estate Commission is appointed by the governor (202 (a)). Realtors, public or real estate licensees have no role in selection.

18. **A) 5**

    The State Real Estate Commission must include five members who shall be a licensed and qualified broker under the existing law (202).

19. **D) The Pennsylvania Real Estate Commission**

    The Pennsylvania Real Estate Commission has the power and authority to administer and enforce the license law (406).

Practice Test 2 – Answers

20. **B) Formulate and enforce the rules by which all real estate licensees must abide**

The Pennsylvania Real Estate Commission administers and enforces laws governing the conduct of licensees (404).

21. **C) Interview consumers who are currently conducting business during the inspection**

No exception in the commission rules for interviewing consumers or members of the public (35.246 (d)). The commission or its authorized representative may interview the broker as well as other licensed or unlicensed employees who work in the office.

22. **B) Issue licenses and registration certificates to persons who comply with provisions established by the license law**

The Pennsylvania Real Estate Commission does not have statutory authority to issue licenses. Licenses are issued by the Department of State (401).

23. **D) Campground membership salesperson**

Campground membership salespersons are required to be licensed and are subject to disciplinary action on the part of the commission (581).

24. **A) The broker protection clause**

A broker may or may not include a broker protection clause; that issue is not addressed by license law. The law requires that a definite termination date be included in an exclusive listing (604 (a)(10)).

25. **D) 75 classroom hours of instruction in courses prescribed by the commission must be completed successfully**

Completion of 75 hours of real estate instruction in areas of study prescribed by the commission is required (521).

26. **A) A broker depositing earnest money into their operating funds**

Comingling of funds, a type of agent misconduct, involves a licensed agent mixing client funds and earnest money with brokerage operating expenses or an agent's personal account. All client money must be kept in a separate account.

27. **C) A random selection of licensees currently active**

The commission cannot investigate a random selection of licensees. The Pennsylvania Real Estate Commission may carry out an investigation of a licensee's conduct upon its own motion as well as upon receipt of a verified complaint in writing from a consumer (604).

Practice Test 2 – Answers

28. **C) The broker may only pay the bonus to a salesperson who is employed by the listing broker**

   License law prohibits a licensed broker from paying compensation to anyone other than his or her licensed employees or another broker, and it prohibits a salesperson from accepting compensation from anyone other than his or her employing broker (604 (a)(12)).

29. **B) Paying a bonus directly to a licensed salesperson employed by another licensed broker**

   License law specifically prohibits a broker from paying a commission or other valuable consideration to anyone other than his or her licensed employees or another real estate broker (604 (a)(12.1)).

30. **A) Before an agreement of sale is executed by the parties**

   The broker must provide each party with a written estimate of reasonably foreseeable expenses associated with the sale that the party may be expected to pay before an agreement of sale is executed (35.334 (a)).

Practice Test 3

Directions:

1. You have a 120-minute time limit for the national portion, and a 60-minute time limit for the state portion.

2. To pass, you must answer at least 60 out of 80 questions correctly on the national portion **AND** at least 23 out of 30 questions on the state portion.

3. Some questions will require mathematics. You may use a calculator.

4. **Phones and pagers are not allowed. Having either will result in automatic dismissal from the exam and nullification of exam scores.**

Tips:

- Answer all questions even if you are unsure.
- Mark any questions you are stuck on and revisit them after you are done. The exam is timed so make sure you finish as many questions as you can.
- After reading the question, try answering it in your head first to avoid getting confused by the choices.
- Read the entire question before looking at the answers.
- Use the process of elimination to filter out choices that don't seem correct to increase your chances of selecting the correct answer.
- Be aware of important keywords like **not, sometimes, always,** and **never.** These words completely alter the ask of the question so it's important to keep track of them.

PLEASE READ THESE INSTRUCTIONS CAREFULLY.

Practice Test 3

Name: _____ Date: _____

NATIONAL PORTION

1. Ⓐ Ⓑ Ⓒ Ⓓ		31. Ⓐ Ⓑ Ⓒ Ⓓ		61. Ⓐ Ⓑ Ⓒ Ⓓ
2. Ⓐ Ⓑ Ⓒ Ⓓ		32. Ⓐ Ⓑ Ⓒ Ⓓ		62. Ⓐ Ⓑ Ⓒ Ⓓ
3. Ⓐ Ⓑ Ⓒ Ⓓ		33. Ⓐ Ⓑ Ⓒ Ⓓ		63. Ⓐ Ⓑ Ⓒ Ⓓ
4. Ⓐ Ⓑ Ⓒ Ⓓ		34. Ⓐ Ⓑ Ⓒ Ⓓ		64. Ⓐ Ⓑ Ⓒ Ⓓ
5. Ⓐ Ⓑ Ⓒ Ⓓ		35. Ⓐ Ⓑ Ⓒ Ⓓ		65. Ⓐ Ⓑ Ⓒ Ⓓ
6. Ⓐ Ⓑ Ⓒ Ⓓ		36. Ⓐ Ⓑ Ⓒ Ⓓ		66. Ⓐ Ⓑ Ⓒ Ⓓ
7. Ⓐ Ⓑ Ⓒ Ⓓ		37. Ⓐ Ⓑ Ⓒ Ⓓ		67. Ⓐ Ⓑ Ⓒ Ⓓ
8. Ⓐ Ⓑ Ⓒ Ⓓ		38. Ⓐ Ⓑ Ⓒ Ⓓ		68. Ⓐ Ⓑ Ⓒ Ⓓ
9. Ⓐ Ⓑ Ⓒ Ⓓ		39. Ⓐ Ⓑ Ⓒ Ⓓ		69. Ⓐ Ⓑ Ⓒ Ⓓ
10. Ⓐ Ⓑ Ⓒ Ⓓ		40. Ⓐ Ⓑ Ⓒ Ⓓ		70. Ⓐ Ⓑ Ⓒ Ⓓ
11. Ⓐ Ⓑ Ⓒ Ⓓ		41. Ⓐ Ⓑ Ⓒ Ⓓ		71. Ⓐ Ⓑ Ⓒ Ⓓ
12. Ⓐ Ⓑ Ⓒ Ⓓ		42. Ⓐ Ⓑ Ⓒ Ⓓ		72. Ⓐ Ⓑ Ⓒ Ⓓ
13. Ⓐ Ⓑ Ⓒ Ⓓ		43. Ⓐ Ⓑ Ⓒ Ⓓ		73. Ⓐ Ⓑ Ⓒ Ⓓ
14. Ⓐ Ⓑ Ⓒ Ⓓ		44. Ⓐ Ⓑ Ⓒ Ⓓ		74. Ⓐ Ⓑ Ⓒ Ⓓ
15. Ⓐ Ⓑ Ⓒ Ⓓ		45. Ⓐ Ⓑ Ⓒ Ⓓ		75. Ⓐ Ⓑ Ⓒ Ⓓ
16. Ⓐ Ⓑ Ⓒ Ⓓ		46. Ⓐ Ⓑ Ⓒ Ⓓ		76. Ⓐ Ⓑ Ⓒ Ⓓ
17. Ⓐ Ⓑ Ⓒ Ⓓ		47. Ⓐ Ⓑ Ⓒ Ⓓ		77. Ⓐ Ⓑ Ⓒ Ⓓ
18. Ⓐ Ⓑ Ⓒ Ⓓ		48. Ⓐ Ⓑ Ⓒ Ⓓ		78. Ⓐ Ⓑ Ⓒ Ⓓ
19. Ⓐ Ⓑ Ⓒ Ⓓ		49. Ⓐ Ⓑ Ⓒ Ⓓ		79. Ⓐ Ⓑ Ⓒ Ⓓ
20. Ⓐ Ⓑ Ⓒ Ⓓ		50. Ⓐ Ⓑ Ⓒ Ⓓ		80. Ⓐ Ⓑ Ⓒ Ⓓ
21. Ⓐ Ⓑ Ⓒ Ⓓ		51. Ⓐ Ⓑ Ⓒ Ⓓ		
22. Ⓐ Ⓑ Ⓒ Ⓓ		52. Ⓐ Ⓑ Ⓒ Ⓓ		
23. Ⓐ Ⓑ Ⓒ Ⓓ		53. Ⓐ Ⓑ Ⓒ Ⓓ		
24. Ⓐ Ⓑ Ⓒ Ⓓ		54. Ⓐ Ⓑ Ⓒ Ⓓ		
25. Ⓐ Ⓑ Ⓒ Ⓓ		55. Ⓐ Ⓑ Ⓒ Ⓓ		
26. Ⓐ Ⓑ Ⓒ Ⓓ		56. Ⓐ Ⓑ Ⓒ Ⓓ		
27. Ⓐ Ⓑ Ⓒ Ⓓ		57. Ⓐ Ⓑ Ⓒ Ⓓ		
28. Ⓐ Ⓑ Ⓒ Ⓓ		58. Ⓐ Ⓑ Ⓒ Ⓓ		
29. Ⓐ Ⓑ Ⓒ Ⓓ		59. Ⓐ Ⓑ Ⓒ Ⓓ		
30. Ⓐ Ⓑ Ⓒ Ⓓ		60. Ⓐ Ⓑ Ⓒ Ⓓ		

Unauthorized copying or reuse of this page is illegal.

Practice Test 3

Name: _____   Date: _____

STATE PORTION

1. Ⓐ Ⓑ Ⓒ Ⓓ
2. Ⓐ Ⓑ Ⓒ Ⓓ
3. Ⓐ Ⓑ Ⓒ Ⓓ
4. Ⓐ Ⓑ Ⓒ Ⓓ
5. Ⓐ Ⓑ Ⓒ Ⓓ
6. Ⓐ Ⓑ Ⓒ Ⓓ
7. Ⓐ Ⓑ Ⓒ Ⓓ
8. Ⓐ Ⓑ Ⓒ Ⓓ
9. Ⓐ Ⓑ Ⓒ Ⓓ
10. Ⓐ Ⓑ Ⓒ Ⓓ
11. Ⓐ Ⓑ Ⓒ Ⓓ
12. Ⓐ Ⓑ Ⓒ Ⓓ
13. Ⓐ Ⓑ Ⓒ Ⓓ
14. Ⓐ Ⓑ Ⓒ Ⓓ
15. Ⓐ Ⓑ Ⓒ Ⓓ
16. Ⓐ Ⓑ Ⓒ Ⓓ
17. Ⓐ Ⓑ Ⓒ Ⓓ
18. Ⓐ Ⓑ Ⓒ Ⓓ
19. Ⓐ Ⓑ Ⓒ Ⓓ
20. Ⓐ Ⓑ Ⓒ Ⓓ
21. Ⓐ Ⓑ Ⓒ Ⓓ
22. Ⓐ Ⓑ Ⓒ Ⓓ
23. Ⓐ Ⓑ Ⓒ Ⓓ
24. Ⓐ Ⓑ Ⓒ Ⓓ
25. Ⓐ Ⓑ Ⓒ Ⓓ
26. Ⓐ Ⓑ Ⓒ Ⓓ
27. Ⓐ Ⓑ Ⓒ Ⓓ
28. Ⓐ Ⓑ Ⓒ Ⓓ
29. Ⓐ Ⓑ Ⓒ Ⓓ
30. Ⓐ Ⓑ Ⓒ Ⓓ

Unauthorized copying or reuse of this page is illegal.

National Portion

1. What is the name given to the estimate amount on a mortgage?

   A. Pre-approval
   B. Post-approval
   C. Principal
   D. Mortgage

2. What is the actual amount of space a tenant can lay carpet and place furniture?

   A. Usable Square Footage
   B. Rentable square footage
   C. Common areas
   D. Service areas

3. What is the name given to an amount of money borrowed to facilitate the purchase of a property?

   A. Escrow
   B. Interest
   C. Down payment
   D. Principal

4. What type of mortgage loan is made available through the United States Department of Veterans Affairs?

   A. Blanket mortgage
   B. Balloon mortgage
   C. Graduated mortgage
   D. VA mortgage

5. What is the value obtained by deducting applied payments from original amortization?

   A. Full term
   B. Paid term
   C. Principal term
   D. Remaining term

6. What is the arrangement that allows a seller to lease a property from a purchaser after selling it?

   A. Leaseback
   B. Leasehold
   C. Sublease
   D. Proprietary lease

7. What type of easement attaches rights to a tenant instead of the land?

   A. Easement appurtenant
   B. Easement in gross
   C. Prescriptive easement
   D. All the above

8. What is the penalty charge for paying back a loan ahead of the scheduled payment plan?

   A. Defaulting penalty
   B. Interest
   C. Prepayment penalty
   D. Principal amount

9. What is an insurance premium paid by the buyer to the lender in order to protect the lender from default on a mortgage?

   A. Hazard insurance
   B. Homeowner's insurance
   C. Private mortgage insurance
   D. Title insurance

10. What is the name given to a party that acts in conjunction with a lender to originate a loan?

    A. Mortgage broker
    B. Third party originator
    C. Lender
    D. Intermediate

11. What is the term used to describe the alteration of a property in order to increase its market value?

    A. Capital Improvement
    B. Preventive maintenance
    C. Appreciation
    D. Common charges

12. What is the tax levied on transfer of property?

    A. Capital gains tax
    B. Deductible tax
    C. Property tax
    D. Transfer tax

13. Which of the following is an appraisal method in real estate?

    A. Sales Comparison Approach
    B. Cost Approach
    C. Income Approach
    D. All of the above

14. For at least how long must an asset be held before being sold to be categorized as long-term capital gains?

    A. One month
    B. Six months
    C. One year
    D. Two years

15. Which of these is considered an operating expense?

    A. Repairs
    B. Depreciation
    C. Payroll
    D. All of the above

16. What is an unlawful detainer?

    A. Forcing rent payments for tenants who have already moved out
    B. Refusing to leave a property despite expiration or termination of lease
    C. Listing a property whose lease has not expired
    D. Subletting a property without permission from the landlord

17. What is the agreement that ensures that the interest rate of a mortgage loan remains unchanged between offer and closing?

    A. Cessation
    B. Amortization
    C. Rate lock
    D. Interest freeze

18. What type of lease gives the tenant an option to purchase the property?

    A. Leaseback
    B. Lease option
    C. Leasehold
    D. Gross lease

19. What is conditioner capacity?

    A. This is the capacity of an air conditioner to heat or cool the room
    B. The space used up by an air conditioner
    C. The strength of an air conditioner
    D. The cooling capacity of an air conditioner and is measured in tons

20. What is the name given to an individual that acts in intermediate for brokers and lenders?

    A. Mortgage broker
    B. Mortgage banker
    C. Attorney
    D. Intermediate

21. If a property is taxed at 30% with a tax levy of $105,000, what is its assessed value?

    A. $136,500
    B. $146,666
    C. $350,000
    D. None of the above

22. What is the notice given when a tenant has a pet in a complex that has no pets policy?

    A. Notice to cure
    B. Notice to quit
    C. Notice of default
    D. Notice of termination

23. What is a roof's vertical rise in inches divided by its horizontal span in feet?

    A. Depth
    B. Width
    C. Pitch
    D. Length

24. Who engages the services of a broker?

    A. The client
    B. The neighbor
    C. The contractor
    D. The appraiser

Practice Test 3 – National Portion

25. Right of way would be best defined as?

   A. Escheat
   B. Easement
   C. Right of ingress
   D. Encumbrance

26. Who can get partial exemptions from property taxes?

   A. Disabled
   B. Schools
   C. Shelters
   D. Markets

27. What age must a person be to get a Real Estate license?

   A. 16 years
   B. 18 years
   C. 30 years
   D. 43 years

28. Which electricity conductor plays the same role as a circuit board?

   A. Cell
   B. Capacitor
   C. Fuse
   D. Switch

29. What is the definition of a bilateral contract?

   A. A contract that involves only the promisor
   B. A contract that involves only the promisee
   C. A contract that involves both a promisor and promisee
   D. A contract that allows both parties to drop all claims and get out of the contract

30. What is real property tax based on?

   A. Assessed value
   B. CMA
   C. Appraisal
   D. Taxable value

31. What agency is responsible for protecting wetlands?

   A. CERCLA
   B. Environmental Protection Agency
   C. FEMA
   D. NY Health Department

32. What is a schedule of the projected future income and expenses for a real estate investment?

   A. IOU
   B. Invoice
   C. Promissory note
   D. Pro Forma Statement

33. What is an agent required to do if a client refuses to sign an agency disclosure form?

    A. Terminate relationship
    B. Create record of refusal in writing
    C. Continue without record of the refusal
    D. Take legal action against the client

34. What is a general voluntary lien?

    A. Mortgage
    B. Taxes
    C. Revenues
    D. Duties

35. If a salesperson's commission is not paid, he resorts to?

    A. Buyer
    B. Seller
    C. Broker
    D. Lender

36. What type of tenancy exists where property is owned by a single individual?

    A. Joint tenancy
    B. Ownership in severalty
    C. Tenancy in entirety
    D. Tenancy in common

37. Who are testers in real estate?

    A. People who pose as real estate clients to check if fair housing is being practiced
    B. People who assess the value of a property
    C. People who pose as borrowers to ensure proper loaning practices
    D. People who approach the seller without the intention of buying

38. What is the term used to describe the natural increase of land?

    A. Expansion
    B. Avulsion
    C. Erosion
    D. Accretion

39. What is the length of time allowed for depreciation for a residential property?

    A. 5 years
    B. 27.5 years
    C. 39 years
    D. 70 years

40. What is the term used to describe personal property?

    A. Chattel
    B. Investment
    C. Possession
    D. Real property

41. Which act was enacted to ensure parties involved in a real estate transaction receive complete settlement cost disclosure?

    A. RESPA
    B. FHA
    C. Clean Water Act
    D. Civil Rights Act

42. What is the name given to the downward movement of water through soil?

    A. Absorption
    B. Filtration
    C. Percolation
    D. Proration

43. What type of income is generated by investing in a limited partnership?

    A. Active income
    B. Passive income
    C. Surplus income
    D. Savings

44. What mortgage type allows the mortgagor to make payments only on the interest accrued?

    A. Blanket mortgage
    B. Balloon mortgage
    C. Graduated mortgage
    D. Straight term mortgage

45. Mary's agent helped her purchase a property and negotiated a mortgage for her. This agent also represented the seller. What type of agent did Mary engage?

    A. Single agent
    B. Dual agent
    C. Double agent
    D. None of the above

46. What is the land survey process that involves the surveyor starting at an easily identifiable point and describing the property in terms of courses and distances and eventually returning to the starting point?

    A. ALTA
    B. Boundary construction
    C. Metes and bounds
    D. Topographic surveys

47. What arrangement allows the seller to absorb an existing loan in order to allow the buyer another mortgage?

    A. Simple mortgage
    B. Wraparound mortgage
    C. Mortgage by conditional sale
    D. Reverse mortgage

48. Which real estate participants are legally required to be licensed?

    A. Sellers
    B. Buyers
    C. Lenders
    D. Real estate agents and brokers

Practice Test 3 – National Portion

49. What is the term used to refer to the act of mixing money belonging to a client with one's own funds?

   A. Commingling
   B. Investing
   C. Stealing
   D. Saving

50. What is the effect of a larger money supply on the interest rates?

   A. They decrease
   B. They increase
   C. Remains constant
   D. They have no relationship

51. What is a homeowner's policy that covers two parts: property and liability?

   A. HO1
   B. HO2
   C. HO3
   D. HO4

52. What is the name given to tax calculated based on the value of an asset?

   A. Ad valorem tax
   B. Property tax
   C. Capital gains tax
   D. Transfer tax

53. What kind of lease agreement requires the landlord to pay for all expenses?

   A. Gross lease
   B. Ground lease
   C. Net lease
   D. Sublease

54. If a seller nets $442,000 from the sale of her home, and the commission is 5%, how much did the home sell for?

   A. $464,100
   B. $420,952
   C. $459,680
   D. None of the above

55. What is the short-term loan that covers the interval between selling one property and buying another?

   A. Bridge Loan
   B. Cash flow
   C. Cash on cash return
   D. Mortgage

56. What are the set rules established for condominium or co-op tenants?

   A. House rules
   B. Investment agreement
   C. Regulations
   D. Policy

Practice Test 3 – National Portion

57. Who is responsible for the rent in a sublease?

    A. New tenant
    B. Lessee
    C. Lessor
    D. Roommate

58. What income type does a salary fall under?

    A. Active income
    B. Passive income
    C. Savings
    D. Investment

59. What is the name given to an estate that gives the holder temporary possession rights?

    A. Concurrent estates
    B. Estate for years
    C. Freehold estates
    D. Leasehold estate

60. What is a permit issued to a builder stating the property is fit for occupancy?

    A. Certificate of occupancy
    B. Contract of sale
    C. Landmark designation
    D. Receipt of sales deposit

61. What kind of mortgage pays off the principal?

    A. Amortized loan
    B. Fixed- rate loan
    C. Floating rate loan
    D. Mortgage

62. What is the income that is left after all operating costs are paid in a real estate investment?

    A. Investment
    B. Net operating income
    C. Profit
    D. Revenue

63. Which lease allows for changes in rent within the lease term?

    A. Graduated lease
    B. Lease break
    C. Sublease
    D. Value point

64. What is the married couple's capital gains tax exclusion on the sale of their primary home?

    A. $50,000
    B. $75,000
    C. $250,000
    D. $500,000

Practice Test 3 – National Portion

65. What should a licensee do with their pocket card?

- A. Advertise it
- B. Carry a physical copy or have a digital image on a device
- C. File it
- D. Use it to get clients

66. You must have a real estate license for all of the following activities **EXCEPT**:

- A. Selling a mobile home not affixed to the land
- B. Selling a commercial property
- C. Selling a residential property
- D. Representing a client who wants to rent

67. What is a single person's capital gains tax exclusion?

- A. $25,000
- B. $100,000
- C. $250,000
- D. $500,000

68. What is the term given to violation of neighbor's property by trespassing?

- A. Easement
- B. Escheat
- C. Encroachment
- D. Encumbrance

69. What type of insurance is referred to as renter's insurance?

- A. HO1
- B. HO2
- C. HO3
- D. HO4

70. What is a form of co-ownership by which all parties have undivided interests in the property but no right of survivorship?

- A. Tenancy in common
- B. Tenancy in entirety
- C. Joint tenancy
- D. Ownership in severalty

71. What conveys a grantor's interest in real property?

- A. Deed
- B. Insurance
- C. Title
- D. Warrant

72. What is the chain of deeds and other documents used in transferring title of land from one owner to another consecutively?

- A. Abstract of title
- B. Deed chain
- C. History of deed
- D. Chain of title

Practice Test 3 – National Portion

73. If you paid a down payment of $200,000 for a property worth $1,000,000 dollars and you currently rent it out for $4,000 a month, what is the cash on cash return?

- A. 4%
- B. 4.8%
- C. 20%
- D. 24%

74. What is a Certificate of Eligibility?

- A. Certificate that shows one is to be exempt from property tax
- B. Certificate that is presented by veterans to show proof that they have met the minimum service requirements to be eligible for a VA loan
- C. Certificate that shows a construction is fit for occupancy
- D. Certificate that shows merit

75. What is the insurance policy that protects a lender from loss due to disputes over ownership of a property and defects in the title?

- A. Hazard insurance
- B. Home warranty
- C. Homeowner's insurance
- D. Title insurance

76. Property that has a divided form of ownership is called?

- A. Cooperative
- B. Planned unit development
- C. Time-share
- D. Joint tenants

77. What is the definition of a syndication?

- A. Income that is earned by a spouse prior to marriage
- B. Land that is divided into smaller pieces of land
- C. Mutual funds that invest in rental properties
- D. Real estate that is purchased by a group which includes at least one sponsor and several investors

78. Which of the following is **not** an essential element of a contract?

- A. Notarized signature
- B. Consideration
- C. Agreement by offer and acceptance
- D. Competent parties

79. Which listing agreement allows the owner of the listed property to sell the property on their own and not have to pay commission to the listing broker?

- A. Open listing
- B. Option listing
- C. Exclusive agency listing
- D. Both A and C

80. What is the listing agreement that gives the broker the payment of commission no matter who sells the property?

- A. Entirety
- B. Exclusive-right-to-sell listing
- C. Open listing
- D. Net Listing

THIS IS THE END OF THE NATIONAL PORTION.

State Portion

1. After a hearing of alleged violation of the law, what action must be taken by the real estate commission?

    A. Impose a fine and suspend license
    B. Suspend license only
    C. Impose a sentence of up to 5 months imprisonment
    D. Impose a fine not exceeding $500

2. When dealing with the public, if a licensee is found guilty of making substantial misrepresentation the commission may?

    A. Impose a jail sentence of up to four months
    B. Impose a fine of up to $8,000
    C. Revoke the licensee's license and/or impose a fine
    D. Suspend the license or impose a fine but not do both

3. Without being properly licensed, an individual was found guilty of engaging in business as a broker/salesperson. The penalty for the first offense includes a fine?

    A. Not exceeding $500 or imprisonment not exceeding three months or both
    B. Of only $100
    C. Of up to $2,000
    D. Of not more than $9,000 and imprisonment for a period not exceeding four years

4. If an individual is found guilty for the second time of engaging in the real estate business without a license, what is the maximum penalty?

    A. Fine of $3,000
    B. Fine of $5,000 and imprisonment for a period of two years
    C. Fine of $9,000 and imprisonment for six years
    D. Imprisonment for three months

Practice Test 3 – State Portion

5. Someone looking to apply for a broker's license must?

    A. Prove that he/she is a high school graduate or provide an education equivalent thereto
    B. Be a U.S. citizen
    C. Be a resident of the Commonwealth of Pennsylvania
    D. Have been active in selling real estate for at least four years

6. A website is developed for advertising the broker's office. What, if anything, does the broker need to include?

    A. Number of revoked licenses
    B. License number of brokerage
    C. No need for any disclosure
    D. Name as it appears on the license

7. Which of the following is legal and **not** cause revocation of the broker's license?

    A. Being declared mentally incompetent for the job
    B. Displaying a "For Sale" sign without the owner's approval
    C. Cheat on the licensing examination
    D. Depositing earnest money received into the firm's escrow account

8. Pennsylvania Real Estate Commission is required to suspend a licensee's license:

    A. If any amount of money had been paid from the Real Estate Recovery Fund to settle a claim against the licensee
    B. If the licensee fails to perform as according to the guaranteed sales plan
    C. If the licensee is slow in processing the property transfer
    D. If the licensee doesn't help the seller to find a potential buyer

9. Which of the following is **not** a violation of license law?

   A. Hiding vital information from the prospective buyer
   B. Putting a "For Sale" sign in front of a house without getting approval from owner
   C. Putting a "For Sale" sign in front of a house after getting approval from owner
   D. Permitting salespersons employed by a broker to maintain their own personal escrow accounts

10. During the advertisement of real property for sale, real estate salespeople?

    A. Should ensure inclusion of the name of the employing broker in the ad
    B. Is required to only include the salesperson's personal phone number
    C. Is required to only include the salesperson's personal address
    D. Is required to specify the location of the property

11. Before reapplying for a license, what is the minimum period of time a licensee must wait if he/she has had their license revoked?

    A. 4 years
    B. 5 years
    C. 6 years
    D. 9 years

12. When a real estate salesperson decides to sell his/her own property, the advertisement should include

    A. Employing broker's name, address and phone number
    B. Is not allowed from advertising as a For Sale by Owner
    C. Specify that she or he is a real estate licensee in the given ad
    D. Does not need to include his or her license status in the ad if the ad is acting as "For Sale by Owner"

13. The broker must also include which of the following, when advertising an individual property for sale?

    A. Personal address information
    B. Company's banking details
    C. Previous property owner's details
    D. The official business name of the broker as indicated on the license

14. Which form of real estate advertisement may have fewer regulatory requirements than others?

    A. Print ads
    B. Text messages
    C. Emails
    D. All real estate advertisements must include the name and contact information of both salesperson and broker of record

15. If an individual wants to sell her own house, then the individual

    A. Does not require a real estate license to sell her house herself
    B. Must first get a real estate license
    C. Needs to hire an attorney
    D. Cannot sell the property by herself

16. For over five years, a salesperson remained inactive without renewal of his license. For getting his/her license reissued, the applicant must

    A. Complete 20 hours of mandatory continuing education with no exam requirement
    B. Complete 50 hours of coursework and pass the salesperson's license exam
    C. Submit to and pass the salesperson's license examination
    D. Just participate in the employing broker's training program

17. What must the broker include in the advertisement when he/she is advertising property for sale?

    A. Price of the property
    B. Salesperson's complete name who secured the listing
    C. Broker's business name designated on the license
    D. None of the above

18. Agents are required to provide a _____ to potential clients, which summarizes the meaning and duties of different kinds of agency.

    A. Pennsylvania mandatory agent-principal disclosure
    B. Agency contract
    C. Consumer notice
    D. Verbal agency consent is sufficient

19. All of the following would be grounds for revoking a broker's license in Pennsylvania state EXCEPT

    A. Agreeing with a seller to accept a listing for more than the company's normal commission rate
    B. Being convicted criminal
    C. Depositing a buyer's money into the employed salesperson's personal checking account
    D. Involved in fraudulent real estate dealings previously

20. In which situation is a licensed agent acting as a limited agent?

    A. When the agent has been designated a specific client by their supervising broker
    B. When the agent represents only one party in a transaction as a seller's or a buyer's agent
    C. When the agent represents its client(s) in only one transaction
    D. When the agent is working solely as a facilitator

21. Who of the following would need to be a licensed real estate broker or salesperson in the state of Pennsylvania?

    A. A seller who wants to sell his/her own property
    B. Property management company comprising of less than three leasing agents
    C. A banker who deals with transactions of real estate matters
    D. A manager employed by an owner to show apartment to potential clients

22. A partnership, association, or corporation will be granted a broker's license under Pennsylvania licensing law, only if?

    A. All members in the brokerage business have broker's license
    B. All license papers are filed with the Secretary of State
    C. Have a net worth of more than $100,000
    D. One partner or officer is appointed as the broker of record

23. In Pennsylvania, if someone wants to apply for a real estate salesperson's license, he/she must?

    A. Is at least 30 years of age
    B. Should be able to prove that the license examination was passed within three years of the date of application
    C. Has completed at least college
    D. Prove that he/she has not been convicted of felony with eight years of applying

24. Upon obtaining an exclusive listing, a broker or licensed salesperson is obligated to

    A. Set up a listing file and issue it a number in compliance with Pennsylvania Real Estate Commission Rules and Regulations
    B. Place advertisements in the local newspapers
    C. Cooperate with every real estate office wishing to participate in the marketing of the listed property
    D. Give the person or persons signing the listing a legible, signed, true, and correct copy

25. Which of the following people applying for a license are **not** required to pass a written exam for the license?

    A. College student
    B. Cemetery salesperson
    C. Marketing agent directly hired by owner
    D. Rental listing referral agent

26. Which situation constitutes designated agency?

    A. A court appoints an agent to sell a house after a court-mandated foreclosure
    B. The owner of a brokerage assigns a former salesperson's client to a different broker
    C. A licensed agent working as both a seller's agent and a buyer's agent
    D. A seller's agent and a buyer's agent both work for the same brokerage

27. Do Pennsylvania property management companies need a real estate broker's license?

    A. Yes
    B. No
    C. Only if they file as an LLC
    D. Only if the tenant wants to buy the property

28. Completion of 14 hours of mandatory continuing education as a condition of license renewal is required by which of the following licensed individuals?

    A. Licensed builder-owner salesperson
    B. Licensed cemetery broker
    C. Licensed campground membership salesperson
    D. Licensed broker of record of a corporation or partnership listing and selling real estate

29. What must be included in the advertisement when a broker advertises his/her production or position in the market?

    A. His/her experience in the relevant field
    B. His/her age
    C. Municipality that the market comprises
    D. Number of associate brokers in his/her agency

30. According to the Real Estate Licensing and Registration Act, how many years can you be inactive before having to reapply for a license?

    A. 2
    B. 3
    C. 4
    D. 5

THIS IS THE END OF THE STATE PORTION.

Practice Test 3 – Answers

Answer Key – National Portion

1.	A	21.	C	41.	A	61.	A
2.	A	22.	A	42.	C	62.	B
3.	D	23.	C	43.	B	63.	A
4.	D	24.	A	44.	D	64.	D
5.	D	25.	B	45.	B	65.	B
6.	A	26.	A	46.	C	66.	A
7.	B	27.	B	47.	B	67.	C
8.	C	28.	C	48.	D	68.	C
9.	C	29.	C	49.	A	69.	D
10.	B	30.	A	50.	A	70.	A
11.	A	31.	B	51.	C	71.	A
12.	D	32.	D	52.	A	72.	D
13.	D	33.	B	53.	A	73.	D
14.	C	34.	A	54.	D	74.	B
15.	D	35.	C	55.	A	75.	D
16.	B	36.	B	56.	A	76.	C
17.	C	37.	A	57.	B	77.	D
18.	B	38.	D	58.	A	78.	A
19.	D	39.	B	59.	D	79.	D
20.	A	40.	A	60.	A	80.	B

1. **A) Pre-approval**

   Prior to purchasing a property, the borrower can visit a lender and obtain a pre-approval letter stating the amount of credit the lender is willing to accord the buyer which will help determine what the buyer can afford.

2. **A) Usable Square Footage**

   Usable square footage is the amount of space you actually occupy in a leased space.

3. **D) Principal**

   The principal is the amount of money that a lender gives a borrower to facilitate property purchase. Payment of principal results in increase in borrower's equity.

4. **D) VA mortgage**

   This is a mortgage plan that is tailored to assist service members and their surviving spouses to become homeowners. There are usually a lot of qualifying standards put in place to be eligible for this type of mortgage and it is usually offered by banks and other credit facilities. The Veteran administration usually acts as a guarantor for the loan. Qualified Veterans are usually eligible for 100% financing.

Practice Test 3 – Answers

5. **D) Remaining term**

   It is usually used to complete the period of time left on a loan and the amount of principal payment to be covered within that period.

6. **A) Leaseback**

   This is an arrangement that allows a seller to lease a property from the purchaser on transfer of ownership. The details surrounding the lease arrangement are usually discussed immediately after the sale.

7. **B) Easement in gross**

   Easement in gross is the agreement that attaches rights to the tenant over the property. Transfer of the land results in an immediate termination of the agreement. The agreement can be renegotiated with the new tenant over time.

8. **C) Prepayment penalty**

   This is the penalty placed on the significant payment of a mortgage within the first five years of the loan. This penalty exists to protect lenders from loss of interest income.

9. **C) Private mortgage insurance**

   These insurance payments are usually discontinued once a buyer builds up to 20% equity on the home.

10. **B) Third party originator.**

    This is any third party used to originate a loan. Lenders often employ the services of third-party moderators to underwrite and originate loans. They offer no ongoing and lasting responsibility for the mortgage.

11. **A) Capital Improvement**

    This is the addition of a permanent change in a structure or restoration of damaged property. It is done to increase the longevity and market value of the property. For an item to be considered a capital investment, it has to be a permanent addition and capable of improving the value of the property.

12. **D) Transfer tax.**

    This is any tax that is levied on transfer of ownership or title of property from one individual to another. It is usually non-deductible. It is usually levied at the local or federal level depending on the type of property changing ownership.

Practice Test 3 – Answers

13. **D) All of the above**

    Sales Comparison Approach, Cost Approach, and Income Approach are all appraisal methods.

14. **C) One year**

    An asset must be held for at least one year before selling in order for profits to be categorized as long-term capital gains.

15. **D) All of the above**

    Operating expenses include any costs associated with the operation and maintenance of an income-producing property.

16. **B) Refusing to leave a property despite expiration or termination of lease**

    Commonly compared to an eviction, which is the legal removal of an individual from a lease due to violation of the terms of the agreement.

17. **C) Rate lock**

    This occurs when lenders lock in a rate because it is the lowest rate being offered at the time. It is not a legally binding agreement and borrowers are allowed to abandon the rates based on the rising and falling.

18. **B) Lease option**

    A lease option is a lease agreement that gives the tenant a choice to purchase the property within or at the end of the lease. It gives the buyer flexibility to make a purchase on the property. Usually involves an upfront agreement between the tenant and the landlord.

19. **D) The cooling capacity of an air conditioner and is measured in tons**

    It is determined by measuring the size of the space being serviced by the air conditioner. The size area of the room is measured and multiplied by 25 BTU to determine the cooling capacity required in an air conditioner.

20. **A) Mortgage broker**

    This is an individual that serves as an intermediate between lenders and brokers. A mortgage broker facilitates negotiations of interest rates and takes circulation of paperwork between the lender and the borrowers.

21. **C) $350,000**

    $105,000 / 0.3 = $350,000

Practice Test 3 – Answers

22. **A) Notice to cure**

    This is a notice given to a leaseholder by the landlord regarding participation in activities that are not allowed in the building. The tenant is given 10 days to correct the mistake. Refusal to make adjustment results in the tenant being served a notice of termination.

23. **C) Pitch**

    Defines the steepness of a roof. It is used to determine the material used for roofing and the space in the attic. It is also used to determine stability so that corrective measures can be undertaken early.

24. **A) The client**

    A broker is required to work in the best interests of the client to ensure the best possible deal for the client.

25. **B) Easement**

    This is the right to use another person's land temporarily without actually possessing it.

26. **A) Disabled**

    Disabled, veterans, elderly, farmers, Gold Star Parents, and Star Program Homeowners. The above classes of people can get partial tax exemption by having the values of their homes reduced translating in reduced property taxes.

27. **B) 18 years**

    This is the minimum required age for a real estate agent that has taken the education course and passed the qualifying exam.

28. **C) Fuse**

    A fuse is a small conductor that is designed to melt under high current to break the circuit. A fuse should always maintain a series connection to the component of the circuit.

29. **C) A contract that involves both a promisor and promisee**

    This contract occurs when both parties exchange a promise for a promise. Both parties enter into an agreement to fulfill their side of the bargain. Each party is also an obligor and obligee in this type of contract.

30. **A) Assessed value**

    Assessed value is the monetary value assigned to a property and is usually used to determine the value of a property for the purpose of taxation.

Practice Test 3 – Answers

31. **B) Environmental Protection Agency**

    The Environmental Protection Agency is tasked with protecting both human and environmental health. The agency creates standards and laws promoting health of individuals and the environment and participates in upholding them by administering correcting efforts like CERCLA.

32. **D) Pro Forma Statement**

    This is an estimate summary of income production if the current trends are maintained. This is usually in multifamily properties in order to help the investor understand general financial operations of the property.

33. **B) Create record of refusal in writing**

    In the case where a client refuses to sign a disclosure, the agent is required to clearly state the names of the client and the facts surrounding the refusal to sign the disclosure. An agent is also required to sign a declaration in the presence of a notary public and have it notarized.

34. **A) Mortgage**

    A voluntary lien is a claim a debtor has over the property of another and is initiated by the debtor as in the case of a mortgage. The debtor cannot legally sell the property as it is considered collateral.

35. **C) Broker**

    An agent resorts to a broker for commission as the law does not allow salespersons to work independently and therefore cannot be paid directly. A broker on receiving commission from the sale of the property is required to split the commission amongst the agents that were involved in the transaction.

36. **B) Ownership in severalty**

    This is a situation where real estate is owned by a single person or entity providing the owner with the most control of the land. A sole owner is at will to take any action on the land such as selling or leasing.

37. **A) People who pose as real estate clients to check if fair housing is being practiced**

    Testing was initiated under the Fair Housing Act to ensure that housing providers act in accordance with the fair housing laws that protect against discrimination based on race, origin and gender.

Practice Test 3 – Answers

38. **D) Accretion**

This is the natural growth of a parcel of land due to mother nature. It occurs due to accumulation of soil on the shoreline of a water body. A decrease due to erosion is also possible.

39. **B) 27.5 years**

Depreciation is the loss of value of a property due to age, wear and tear. A residential property can only declare depreciation after 27.5 years in order to reduce the value of the property and property tax on the property.

40. **A) Chattel**

A chattel is a tangible property which is either mobile or immobile. However, this term cannot be used to describe real estate holdings.

41. **A) RESPA**

The Real Estate Settling Procedures Act was developed in order to protect the parties involved in a real estate transaction from abuse during the settlement process. The act mandates lenders and brokers to disclose all matters crucial to the transaction service, settlement service and consumer protection laws

42. **C) Percolation**

This is the process in which water reaches the subsoil and roots. The pore space present in soil acts as a medium for the water to percolate. The ability of water to move through soil is dependent on the soil texture and structure. Some soils allow water to move very deep into the ground which may result in mixing with underground water reservoirs.

43. **B) Passive income**

This is income that is generated with minimal activity. It requires little to no effort to earn on a daily basis.

44. **D) Straight term mortgage**

A straight term mortgage is a mortgage that allows the mortgagor to make monthly payments on the interest accrued throughout the mortgage's lifespan. The principal remains unpaid until a set date where it becomes due for payment in full.

45. **B) Dual agent**

Mary's agent was able to perform the above transactions for her because he was working for both the Mary and the seller of the property.

Practice Test 3 – Answers

46. **C) Metes and bounds**

    This is a legal principle of land description and uses natural and artificial landmarks as boundaries. It is often used to describe irregular tracts of land. Metes defines straight line distances while bounds defines a less regular but identifiable lines. Measurements from an original point that is a monument and metes and bounds are described taking into account the boundaries. The process is repeated until the surveyor returns to the original point.

47. **B) Wraparound mortgage**

    Wraparound mortgages are used to refinance property. They are mini loans that include the balance of the preexisting mortgage and an additional loan to cover the new property. The seller is granted a promissory note highlighting the amount due.

48. **D) Real estate agents and brokers**

    They need to be licensed as they legally represent clients, buyers and sellers, in transferring ownership of property.

49. **A) Commingling**

    This is a breach of trust that occurs when a representative of a client mixes individual funds with that of the client making it impossible to determine the amounts that belong to each individual.

50. **A) They decrease**

    Money supply is influenced by supply and demand. An increase in the money supply will result in a decreased interest rate making it easier to borrow and vice versa. Therefore, money and interest rates have an inversely proportional relationship.

51. **C) HO3**

    A home owner's policy is a property insurance that covers losses and damages done to the insured's house and assets within the home. It also provides liability coverage against accidents within the home.

52. **A) Ad valorem tax**

    This is the tax levied by a municipality or local government entity based on assessed value. A public assessor is engaged to value the property in order to calculate the tax owed.

53. **A) Gross lease**

    This is a flat rent fee that included all expenses associated with ownership. It is inclusive of incidental charges such as taxes, insurance and utilities. It is an uncommon lease as landlords are unaware of the utility charges that may be incurred by a tenant.

Practice Test 3 – Answers

54. **D) None of the above**

    $442,000 / (1 - 0.05) = $465,263

55. **A) Bridge Loan**

    This is a short-term loan of up to one year that provides cash flow enabling an individual to meet current obligations while awaiting permanent financing. It is often used in real estate to purchase a new home while awaiting the sale of the old property.

56. **A) House rules**

    These are set rules that have been put in place to ensure the comfort of the tenants living within the building. Violation of the house rules clause may result in eviction.

57. **B) Lessee**

    The original tenant for rent as he/she is liable to the owner. In case of overdue rent by the new tenant, the original tenant is held accountable.

58. **A) Active income**

    This is an income earned from performing services. Active participation is required to yield payment.

59. **D) Leasehold estate**

    This is a lease that allows the tenant to have real property for an extended period of time. A time frame is agreed upon in the lease and the tenant is allowed to erect structures and profit from the business that has been established at the site.

60. **A) Certificate of occupancy**

    This is a legal statement issued by the building department clearing a building for occupancy on meeting the building codes and other laws that surround the construction of a residential or commercial building. It can be obtained when a new building is constructed or an old building is repurposed.

61. **A) Amortized loan**

    An amortized loan is a loan with a scheduled payment over a period of time that pays off the interest and principal. An amortized loan payment schedule focuses on paying off the interest and progresses into the principal.

Practice Test 3 – Answers

62. **B) Net operating income**

    This is a method used to value the income generating properties. To obtain the value, all expenses incurred during operations is subtracted to the total income produced by the property. To get the true value produced by the property, revenues earned must be included.

63. **A) Graduated lease**

    A graduated lease is an agreement between the landlord and tenant that allows for periodic adjustment of monthly payments based on the market value of the property. It stands to benefit the landlord over a long period of time.

64. **D) $500,000**

    In accordance with the Taxpayers Relief Act, a married couple is eligible for exclusion from capital gain tax for profits of up to $500,000. This is provided the property sold is a primary residence, they have been living in it for at least 2 years.

65. **B) Carry a physical copy or have a digital image on a device**

    A pocket card is a pocket-sized license identifying the holder as a licensed agent. It contains a photo, name and business address of the holder.

66. **A) Selling a mobile home not affixed to the land**

    If the mobile home is sitting on a leased lot, then it is considered as personal property and can therefore be sold like a car or other personal belongings.

67. **C) $250,000**

    According to the Taxpayers relief act, a single person is eligible for a capital gains tax exemption for profits of up to $250,000 on the sale of a primary home.

68. **C) Encroachment**

    Encroachment is a violation of property rights that occurs when an individual chooses to ignore set boundaries. This can be by extending structure into the neighbor's land or illegally entering the neighbor's property.

69. **D) HO4**

    This insurance is designed to protect the insured and belongings from the covered losses. It covers liability, personal property, additional living expenses and medical payments to others. The insurance covers against risks specified in the policy.

Practice Test 3 – Answers

70. **A) Tenancy in common**

    A tenancy in common is a legal agreement where two or more people with undivided rights own a property. Members of a tenancy in common are not mandated to have equal rights and can enter the agreement at any time. Members of a tenancy in common are free to leave their shares to a beneficiary.

71. **A) Deed**

    This is a signed legal document that conveys interest of a property and is used in cases of transfer of property provided a set of conditions are met. For a deed to hold legal merit, it must be filed in a public record.

72. **D) Chain of title**

    This is an official ownership record of a property. It is usually maintained from a centralized registry. It is used widely to protect lenders and buyers from losses occurring due to errors in the title report.

73. **D) 24%**

    ($4,000 * 12) / $200,000 = 0.24

74. **B) Certificate that is presented by veterans to show proof that they have met the minimum service requirements to be eligible for a VA loan**

    The Certificate of Eligibility serves as proof of a veteran's military service and must be provided to lenders during the VA loan process

75. **D) Title insurance**

    A title insurance is based on the indemnity clause. It is taken by a buyer to protect the lender from loss caused by unidentified defects in the title. It acts against traditional insurance by protecting clients against claims on a past occurrence

76. **C) Time-share**

    Also called vacation ownership, a time-share is shared ownership of a property. This type of property is typically a vacation property i.e. a condominium in a resort area. The buyer typically purchases a certain period of time for the unit, typically one- to two-week periods.

77. **D) Real estate that is purchased by a group which includes at least one sponsor and several investors**

    Syndication is a method investors can use to invest in properties. Investors pool their financial and intellectual resources together to invest in properties that they would not be able to invest in individually.

Practice Test 3 – Answers

78. **A) Notarized signature**

    A notarized signature is not necessary in a contract. A legal purpose, competent parties, offer and acceptance, consideration and consent are the essential elements of a contract.

79. **D) Both A and C**

    Exclusive agency listing is an agreement between a real estate firm and seller which grants the firm the exclusive rights to sell the property but also allows the seller to sell the home without paying a commission to the listing agent. An open listing is a property listing using multiple real estate agents. This type of listing also allows an owner to list and sell the property without paying a commission to an agent.

80. **B) Exclusive-right-to-sell listing**

    A legal agreement under which the seller agrees to pay a commission to the listing broker. The listing broker acts as the agent and is provided commission whether the property is sold through the listing broker, seller or anyone else. An exception occurs when the seller names one or more individuals/entities as exemptions in the listing agreement.

Practice Test 3 – Answers

Answer Key – State Portion

1.	A	21.	B
2.	C	22.	D
3.	A	23.	B
4.	B	24.	D
5.	A	25.	B
6.	D	26.	D
7.	D	27.	A
8.	A	28.	D
9.	C	29.	C
10.	A	30.	D
11.	B		
12.	C		
13.	D		
14.	B		
15.	A		
16.	C		
17.	C		
18.	C		
19.	A		
20.	C		

1. **A) Impose a fine and suspend license**

   As a result of a hearing, the commission may decide to suspend or revoke a license as well as impose fines not exceeding $1,000 (604 (a)).

2. **C) Revoke the licensee's license and/or impose a fine**

   The commission may suspend or revoke a license or impose a fine of up to $1,000 or do both if a licensee is found guilty of making any substantial misrepresentation. The commission does not have authority to impose a jail sentence (604 (a)).

3. **A) Not exceeding $500 or imprisonment not exceeding three months or both**

   License law provides that any person who engages in business without being licensed is subject to criminal prosecution. The first offense is a summary offense punishable by a fine not exceeding $500, imprisonment not exceeding three months, or both (303).

4. **B) Fine of $5,000 and imprisonment for a period of two years**

   The maximum penalty would be a fine of $5,000 and imprisonment for a period of two years. Specifically, the penalty for conviction for a second or subsequent offense is a fine of not less than $2,000 but not more than $5,000, imprisonment for not less than one year but not more than two years, or both (303).

Practice Test 3 – Answers

5. **A) Prove that he/she is a high school graduate or provide an education equivalent thereto**

   Upon conviction for a first offense for practicing real estate without a license, the maximum penalty is a fine not exceeding $500, imprisonment not exceeding three months, or both (303).

6. **D) Name as it appears on the license**

   The real estate commission policy regarding internet advertising requires that the broker's name as it appears on the license must be included on each page of the site on which the firm's advertisement occurs.

7. **D) Depositing earnest money received into the firm's escrow account**

   The broker is required to deposit earnest money into an escrow account. Erecting a "For Sale" sign without written consent is a violation of 604 (a)(8).

8. **A) If any amount of money had been paid from the Real Estate Recovery Fund to settle a claim against the licensee**

   Issue that requires an automatic suspension of the license is when the commission pays money from the recovery fund to settle a claim against a licensee (803(f)).

9. **C) Putting a "For Sale" sign in front of a house after getting approval from owner**

   A broker may place a "For Sale" sign on a property after receiving permission to do so. Brokers may not engage in discriminatory conduct (604(a)(22)).

10. **A) Should ensure inclusion of the name of the employing broker in the ad**

    An advertisement by a salesperson must contain the business name and telephone number of the employing broker (3 5.3 05 (b)).

11. **B) 5 years**

    Any person whose license has been revoked may reapply at the end of a five-year period from the date of revocation (501(c)).

12. **C) Specify that she or he is a real estate licensee in the given ad**

    License status in advertisements for property is required to be disclosed, if the property is not listed for sale with a real estate company (35.304).

13. **D) The official business name of the broker as indicated on the license**

    The business name as designated on the license must be included in all advertising (35.305).

Practice Test 3 – Answers

14. **B) Text messages**

    Unlike print ads, yard signs, website ads, and emails, text message ads are only required to contain the name of the real estate salesperson, as long as they are not part of a blanket text campaign

15. **A) Does not require a real estate license to sell her house herself**

    Owners of real estate conducting business with respect to their own property are not required to be licensed. They are excluded from licensure (304 (1)).

16. **C) Submit to and pass the salesperson's license examination**

    If someone remains inactive for over 5 years with their license being renewed, they must pass the license examination prior to having their license reissued.

17. **C) Broker's business name designated on the license**

    A broker is required to advertise under the business name designated on the license (35.305).

18. **C) Consumer notice**

    Licensed real estate agents must provide a consumer notice to potential clients. Though not a legal contract, by Pennsylvania law agents are required to provide this document, which ensures that clients are fully informed about the nature of the relationship they are creating.

19. **A) Agreeing with a seller to accept a listing for more than the company's normal commission rate**

    A broker's compensation can be discussed and changed between the parties. Misleading advertising is prohibited under 604 (a)(5) and being convicted of a felony could result in revocation of the broker's license under 604 (a)(14).

20. **C) When the agent represents its client(s) in only one transaction**

    Limited agency, also known as special agency, is a situation in Pennsylvania where a licensed agent represents a client or clients in a specific transaction or series of transactions. This form of agency is not ongoing and does not include special privileges for the agent on behalf of the client.

21. **B) Property management company comprising of less than three leasing agents**

    Managing real estate is an activity included in the definition of a real estate broker provided in the license law, so a company will need a license (201).

Practice Test 3 – Answers

22. **D) One partner or officer is appointed as the broker of record**

    Corporations, partnerships, and associations can be issued a broker's license if the individual appointed as the broker of record fulfils all the requirements for issuance of a broker's license.

23. **B) Should be able to prove that the license examination was passed within three years of the date of application**

    Sections 521 and 522 establish requirements, which include that the application shall be received by the commission within three years of the date upon which the applicant passed the examination.

24. **D) Give the person or persons signing the listing a legible, signed, true, and correct copy**

    License law requires the licensee to furnish a copy of the listing to all signatories at the time of execution (604 (a)(9)).

25. **B) Cemetery salesperson**

    There is no examination or coursework required for a cemetery salesperson.

26. **D) A seller's agent and a buyer's agent both work for the same brokerage**

    In designated agency, a seller's agent and a buyer's agent both work for the same brokerage. This is referred to as designated agency because this situation often occurs to avoid a case of dual agency, where the same agent is working for both parties. The supervising broker then assigns another agent from the brokerage to one of the parties.

27. **A) Yes**

    Any property manager who leases, lists or manages real estate will need a broker's license to carry out such services.

28. **D) Licensed broker of record of a corporation or partnership listing and selling real estate**

    The requirements for mandatory continuing education requirements apply to real estate brokers and real estate salespersons only.

29. **C) Municipality that the market comprises**

    Advertisements by a broker about production or position in the market must identify the municipality that the market comprises (35.307 (b)).

Practice Test 3 – Answers

30. **D) 5**

Any person whose license has been revoked may reapply at the end of a five-year period from the date of revocation. They must meet all of the licensing qualifications of the act, including the examination requirement (501(c)).

Practice Test 4

Directions:

1. You have a 120-minute time limit for the national portion, and a 60-minute time limit for the state portion.

2. To pass, you must answer at least 60 out of 80 questions correctly on the national portion **AND** at least 23 out of 30 questions on the state portion.

3. Some questions will require mathematics. You may use a calculator.

4. **Phones and pagers are not allowed. Having either will result in automatic dismissal from the exam and nullification of exam scores.**

Tips:

- Answer all questions even if you are unsure.
- Mark any questions you are stuck on and revisit them after you are done. The exam is timed so make sure you finish as many questions as you can.
- After reading the question, try answering it in your head first to avoid getting confused by the choices.
- Read the entire question before looking at the answers.
- Use the process of elimination to filter out choices that don't seem correct to increase your chances of selecting the correct answer.
- Be aware of important keywords like **not, sometimes, always,** and **never.** These words completely alter the ask of the question so it's important to keep track of them.

PLEASE READ THESE INSTRUCTIONS CAREFULLY.

Practice Test 4

Name: _____ Date: _____

NATIONAL PORTION

1. Ⓐ Ⓑ Ⓒ Ⓓ	31. Ⓐ Ⓑ Ⓒ Ⓓ	61. Ⓐ Ⓑ Ⓒ Ⓓ	
2. Ⓐ Ⓑ Ⓒ Ⓓ	32. Ⓐ Ⓑ Ⓒ Ⓓ	62. Ⓐ Ⓑ Ⓒ Ⓓ	
3. Ⓐ Ⓑ Ⓒ Ⓓ	33. Ⓐ Ⓑ Ⓒ Ⓓ	63. Ⓐ Ⓑ Ⓒ Ⓓ	
4. Ⓐ Ⓑ Ⓒ Ⓓ	34. Ⓐ Ⓑ Ⓒ Ⓓ	64. Ⓐ Ⓑ Ⓒ Ⓓ	
5. Ⓐ Ⓑ Ⓒ Ⓓ	35. Ⓐ Ⓑ Ⓒ Ⓓ	65. Ⓐ Ⓑ Ⓒ Ⓓ	
6. Ⓐ Ⓑ Ⓒ Ⓓ	36. Ⓐ Ⓑ Ⓒ Ⓓ	66. Ⓐ Ⓑ Ⓒ Ⓓ	
7. Ⓐ Ⓑ Ⓒ Ⓓ	37. Ⓐ Ⓑ Ⓒ Ⓓ	67. Ⓐ Ⓑ Ⓒ Ⓓ	
8. Ⓐ Ⓑ Ⓒ Ⓓ	38. Ⓐ Ⓑ Ⓒ Ⓓ	68. Ⓐ Ⓑ Ⓒ Ⓓ	
9. Ⓐ Ⓑ Ⓒ Ⓓ	39. Ⓐ Ⓑ Ⓒ Ⓓ	69. Ⓐ Ⓑ Ⓒ Ⓓ	
10. Ⓐ Ⓑ Ⓒ Ⓓ	40. Ⓐ Ⓑ Ⓒ Ⓓ	70. Ⓐ Ⓑ Ⓒ Ⓓ	
11. Ⓐ Ⓑ Ⓒ Ⓓ	41. Ⓐ Ⓑ Ⓒ Ⓓ	71. Ⓐ Ⓑ Ⓒ Ⓓ	
12. Ⓐ Ⓑ Ⓒ Ⓓ	42. Ⓐ Ⓑ Ⓒ Ⓓ	72. Ⓐ Ⓑ Ⓒ Ⓓ	
13. Ⓐ Ⓑ Ⓒ Ⓓ	43. Ⓐ Ⓑ Ⓒ Ⓓ	73. Ⓐ Ⓑ Ⓒ Ⓓ	
14. Ⓐ Ⓑ Ⓒ Ⓓ	44. Ⓐ Ⓑ Ⓒ Ⓓ	74. Ⓐ Ⓑ Ⓒ Ⓓ	
15. Ⓐ Ⓑ Ⓒ Ⓓ	45. Ⓐ Ⓑ Ⓒ Ⓓ	75. Ⓐ Ⓑ Ⓒ Ⓓ	
16. Ⓐ Ⓑ Ⓒ Ⓓ	46. Ⓐ Ⓑ Ⓒ Ⓓ	76. Ⓐ Ⓑ Ⓒ Ⓓ	
17. Ⓐ Ⓑ Ⓒ Ⓓ	47. Ⓐ Ⓑ Ⓒ Ⓓ	77. Ⓐ Ⓑ Ⓒ Ⓓ	
18. Ⓐ Ⓑ Ⓒ Ⓓ	48. Ⓐ Ⓑ Ⓒ Ⓓ	78. Ⓐ Ⓑ Ⓒ Ⓓ	
19. Ⓐ Ⓑ Ⓒ Ⓓ	49. Ⓐ Ⓑ Ⓒ Ⓓ	79. Ⓐ Ⓑ Ⓒ Ⓓ	
20. Ⓐ Ⓑ Ⓒ Ⓓ	50. Ⓐ Ⓑ Ⓒ Ⓓ	80. Ⓐ Ⓑ Ⓒ Ⓓ	
21. Ⓐ Ⓑ Ⓒ Ⓓ	51. Ⓐ Ⓑ Ⓒ Ⓓ		
22. Ⓐ Ⓑ Ⓒ Ⓓ	52. Ⓐ Ⓑ Ⓒ Ⓓ		
23. Ⓐ Ⓑ Ⓒ Ⓓ	53. Ⓐ Ⓑ Ⓒ Ⓓ		
24. Ⓐ Ⓑ Ⓒ Ⓓ	54. Ⓐ Ⓑ Ⓒ Ⓓ		
25. Ⓐ Ⓑ Ⓒ Ⓓ	55. Ⓐ Ⓑ Ⓒ Ⓓ		
26. Ⓐ Ⓑ Ⓒ Ⓓ	56. Ⓐ Ⓑ Ⓒ Ⓓ		
27. Ⓐ Ⓑ Ⓒ Ⓓ	57. Ⓐ Ⓑ Ⓒ Ⓓ		
28. Ⓐ Ⓑ Ⓒ Ⓓ	58. Ⓐ Ⓑ Ⓒ Ⓓ		
29. Ⓐ Ⓑ Ⓒ Ⓓ	59. Ⓐ Ⓑ Ⓒ Ⓓ		
30. Ⓐ Ⓑ Ⓒ Ⓓ	60. Ⓐ Ⓑ Ⓒ Ⓓ		

Unauthorized copying or reuse of this page is illegal.

Practice Test 4

Name: _____   Date: _____

STATE PORTION

1. Ⓐ Ⓑ Ⓒ Ⓓ
2. Ⓐ Ⓑ Ⓒ Ⓓ
3. Ⓐ Ⓑ Ⓒ Ⓓ
4. Ⓐ Ⓑ Ⓒ Ⓓ
5. Ⓐ Ⓑ Ⓒ Ⓓ
6. Ⓐ Ⓑ Ⓒ Ⓓ
7. Ⓐ Ⓑ Ⓒ Ⓓ
8. Ⓐ Ⓑ Ⓒ Ⓓ
9. Ⓐ Ⓑ Ⓒ Ⓓ
10. Ⓐ Ⓑ Ⓒ Ⓓ
11. Ⓐ Ⓑ Ⓒ Ⓓ
12. Ⓐ Ⓑ Ⓒ Ⓓ
13. Ⓐ Ⓑ Ⓒ Ⓓ
14. Ⓐ Ⓑ Ⓒ Ⓓ
15. Ⓐ Ⓑ Ⓒ Ⓓ
16. Ⓐ Ⓑ Ⓒ Ⓓ
17. Ⓐ Ⓑ Ⓒ Ⓓ
18. Ⓐ Ⓑ Ⓒ Ⓓ
19. Ⓐ Ⓑ Ⓒ Ⓓ
20. Ⓐ Ⓑ Ⓒ Ⓓ
21. Ⓐ Ⓑ Ⓒ Ⓓ
22. Ⓐ Ⓑ Ⓒ Ⓓ
23. Ⓐ Ⓑ Ⓒ Ⓓ
24. Ⓐ Ⓑ Ⓒ Ⓓ
25. Ⓐ Ⓑ Ⓒ Ⓓ
26. Ⓐ Ⓑ Ⓒ Ⓓ
27. Ⓐ Ⓑ Ⓒ Ⓓ
28. Ⓐ Ⓑ Ⓒ Ⓓ
29. Ⓐ Ⓑ Ⓒ Ⓓ
30. Ⓐ Ⓑ Ⓒ Ⓓ

Unauthorized copying or reuse of this page is illegal.

National Portion

1. Which of the following is considered commercial real estate?

   A. Office building
   B. Warehouse
   C. Multifamily house
   D. All of the above

2. Jack is trying to convince Mary to move to a particular neighborhood because the residents there are of her ethnic background and religion. What is guilty of?

   A. Blockbusting
   B. Discriminating
   C. Convincing
   D. Steering

3. What type of lease would a tenant take when using a warehouse for the purpose of manufacturing and distribution?

   A. Gross lease
   B. Net lease
   C. Percentage lease
   D. Proprietary lease

4. What is a notice given on a pending lawsuit?

   A. Lis Pendens
   B. Statute of limitations
   C. Notice of intent
   D. Notice of default

5. Who issues variances?

   A. Architectural Review Board
   B. EPA
   C. Municipal Engineers
   D. Zoning Board of Appeals

6. What is the name given to an individual who originates, sells and services mortgage loans?

   A. Mortgage Banker
   B. Mortgage Broker
   C. Lender
   D. Borrower

7. What is the exterior layer of a house?

   A. Eaves
   B. Flashing
   C. Pitch
   D. Sheathing

8. Who holds on to the security deposit?

   A. Agent
   B. Broker
   C. Buyer
   D. Landlord

9. What is the term used to define the estimated age of a property based on its utilities and physical wear and tear?

   A. Economic life
   B. Effective age
   C. Use discount
   D. Depreciation

10. How long are brokers required to hold on to property files?

    A. One year
    B. Three years
    C. Five years
    D. Never

11. What is the unit used to measure furnace or air conditioner capacity?

    A. British Thermal Unit
    B. Bytes
    C. Joules
    D. Watts

12. What describes the type of estate granted within a lease?

    A. Acceleration clause
    B. Annuity law
    C. Cancellation clause
    D. Habendum clause

13. What type of income is income generated from a rental property?

    A. Active
    B. Passive
    C. Portfolio
    D. All the above

14. What is another name used to refer to land lease?

    A. Ground lease
    B. Home lease
    C. Percentage lease
    D. Estate lease

15. Which regulations govern the construction details of buildings with the sole interest of safeguarding the occupants and general public?

    A. APR
    B. Building codes
    C. Leasing laws
    D. Zoning codes

16. If a seller nets $325,000 from the sale of her home, and the commission is 3%, how much did the home sell for?

    A. $334,750
    B. $335,051
    C. $315,250
    D. $334,027

Practice Test 4 – National Portion

17. Personal property that is attached to real property, such as a chandelier, is regarded as

- A. An emblement
- B. An appliance
- C. A fixture
- D. A liability

18. What are outside amenities that maximize use of property called?

- A. Cosmetic improvements
- B. Essential improvements
- C. Offsite improvements
- D. Supplemental improvements

19. Which form of ownership passes the shares of ownership upon death?

- A. Life estate
- B. Severalty
- C. Tenancy in common
- D. Joint tenancy

20. If a property manager is fixing a leaky pipe, what type of maintenance is he doing?

- A. Aesthetic maintenance
- B. Appreciation
- C. Breakdown prevention
- D. Preventive maintenance

21. Which act was enacted in order to identify hazardous sites?

- A. Americans with disabilities Act
- B. CERCLA
- C. Fair Housing Act
- D. Civil Rights Act

22. What is tenancy in common?

- A. A shared tenancy in which each holder has a distinct, separately transferable interest
- B. A tenancy in which each holder has equal interest, where interest is automatically passed in case of death
- C. A tenancy in which interest is returned to the public upon death
- D. A tenancy in which a single owner owns full ownership of a property

23. What is the money available after deducting all expenses?

- A. Cash out returns
- B. Cash flow
- C. Cash on cash return
- D. Revenue

24. What is an involuntary lien?

- A. A lien that arises without the property owner's consent
- B. A lien that is initiated with owner's consent
- C. A lien that cannot be cashed on
- D. None of the above

25. What is the name given to property that legally qualifies as owner's principal property?

    A. Commercial property
    B. Homestead property
    C. Real property
    D. Personal property

26. A person authorized to handle a principal's affairs in one specific area is referred to as?

    A. General agent
    B. Dual agent
    C. Multi agent
    D. Special agent

27. What are real property rights conferred with ownership?

    A. Bundle of rights
    B. Right of first refusal
    C. Riparian rights
    D. Doctrine of equitable conversion

28. What is the fine placed for a violation of license law?

    A. $1,000
    B. $5,000
    C. $6,000
    D. $10,000

29. What is the term for commercial property depreciation?

    A. 5 years
    B. 29 years
    C. 39 years
    D. 40 years

30. The division of expenses at the time of closing between the buyer and seller in proportion to the actual use of a property is called?

    A. Bill of sale
    B. Loan to value ratio
    C. Proration
    D. Tax abatement

31. What is the equivalent of 1 cubic foot?

    A. 5.25 gallons
    B. 7.26 gallons
    C. 7.48 gallons
    D. 10 gallons

32. What is a statement that shows total revenues generated based on rent rolls and management styles?

    A. Invoice statement
    B. Income statement
    C. Pro forma statement
    D. Operating statement

33. What type of building is divided into two condominiums where the first is the co-op residential units (80%) and the second is for professional/commercial units (20%)?

    A. Condo
    B. Condop
    C. Co-op
    D. Multi family home

34. A person authorized to handle a principal's affairs in more than one specific area is referred to as?

    A. Special agent
    B. General Agent
    C. Dual agent
    D. Broker

35. What are the laws that limit the maximum interest rate that can be charged?

    A. APR
    B. Annuity laws
    C. FHA
    D. Usury

36. What is the nature of the title in co-op ownership?

    A. Freehold
    B. Leasehold
    C. Regular hold
    D. Lease assignment

37. What is a non-possessory interest in property giving a lienholder the right to foreclose?

    A. Mortgage
    B. Duties
    C. Taxes
    D. Revenue

38. What is the agreement that allows the tenant to continue living on a property once the lease has expired?

    A. Tenancy in common
    B. Tenancy in entirety
    C. Tenancy in sufferance
    D. Ownership in severalty

39. Can a salesperson hold other jobs?

    A. Yes
    B. No
    C. Only if it is in real estate
    D. Maybe

40. What does the Secondary Mortgage Market refer to in the loan process?

    A. Buyers that buy houses on mortgage
    B. Sellers that offer buy down arrangement
    C. Lending market
    D. Private investors and government agencies that buy and sell real estate mortgages

Practice Test 4 – National Portion

41. What are air rights?

    A. Right to breath
    B. Right to own an airspace
    C. Right to package air
    D. Rights granted to a property owner on the vertical space above the property

42. What is the relationship where agents work together in the best interest of their respective clients?

    A. Dual agency
    B. Single agency
    C. Co-broking
    D. Co-borrowing

43. What is the legal term for passing responsibility of your apartment onto another tenant?

    A. Sub lease
    B. Lease assignment
    C. Leasehold
    D. Lease break

44. If you have a loan of $200,000 with a 12% interest, how much do you pay in interest every month?

    A. $1,200
    B. $2,000
    C. $2,400
    D. $24,000

45. What are the extra charges above the selling costs that are incurred by the buyer on the purchase of a home?

    A. Common costs
    B. Closing costs
    C. Down payment
    D. Short fall

46. What are the monthly charges imposed on condo tenants?

    A. Common charges
    B. Common costs
    C. Service fees
    D. Short fall

47. What is the name given to the ratio defined by dividing monthly debt payments to gross monthly income?

    A. Loan to value ratio
    B. Debt to income ratio
    C. Earnest money deposit
    D. Foreclosure

48. What is the percentage amount of the selling price that is deposited by the buyer when closing a real estate transaction?

    A. Down payment
    B. Escrow
    C. Earnest money deposit
    D. Tax abatement

49. What is earnest money deposit?

    A. Money deposited by the buyer to the seller to show interest in the purchase of a home
    B. Purchase money
    C. Down payment
    D. Security deposit

50. What is the financial agreement that allows a third party to regulate payment where two parties are involved?

    A. Security deposit
    B. Sales deposit
    C. Escrow
    D. Earnest money deposit

51. What is the notice given when a tenant is in violation of the lease agreement and is up for eviction?

    A. Notice to cure
    B. Notice of intention
    C. Notice of termination
    D. Notice to quit

52. What is the notice given when a squatter is accommodated without the landlord's consent?

    A. Notice of default
    B. Notice of intention
    C. Notice to cure
    D. Notice to quit

53. What is the notice given to state that no work has been performed?

    A. Notice of cessation
    B. Notice given to evict an unruly tenant
    C. Notice filed in court by a lender on defaulting of payment
    D. Notice to discontinue the breach of lease within 10 days

54. What is the name given to a visit made to a potential property to identify the condition of the house?

    A. Final walk through
    B. Home inspection
    C. Appraisal
    D. Assessment

55. What mortgage plan allows a borrower to switch to a fixed-rate mortgage?

    A. Adjustable Rate Mortgage
    B. Convertible ARM
    C. Fixed rate mortgage
    D. Floating rate mortgage

56. What is the situation that arises when an individual that is legally required to make payments does not fulfill this obligation?

    A. Delinquency
    B. Defaulting
    C. Escalation clause
    D. Foreclosure

57. Which agency insures FHA-approved lenders?

    A. CERCLA
    B. Consumer Financial Protection Bureau
    C. Federal Emergency Management Agency
    D. Federal Housing Administration

58. Which agency is commissioned with overseeing products and services offered to consumers in the finance industry?

    A. Consumer Financial Protection Bureau
    B. Federal Housing Administration
    C. Environmental Protection Agency
    D. Federal Emergency Management Agency

59. What service allows brokers to share their listings?

    A. Broker Listing Service
    B. Single Agency Listing
    C. Multiple Listing Service
    D. Shared Listing Service

60. What is the contract covering household maintenance systems?

    A. Deed
    B. Home warranty
    C. Hazard insurance
    D. HO4

61. What is the name given to a real estate transaction where buyers outbid each other for the property?

    A. Acceleration clause
    B. Escalation clause
    C. Public auction
    D. Tender

62. What is the name given to a notice given showing interest in a property?

    A. Notice of cessation
    B. Notice to cure
    C. Notice of default
    D. Notice of intent

63. What is the increase in the value of a property?

    A. Appreciation
    B. Depreciation
    C. Obsolescence
    D. All of the above

64. What is the mortgage payment plan that involves making payments every fortnight?

    A. Balloon mortgage
    B. Biweekly mortgage
    C. Blanket mortgage
    D. Graduated mortgage

65. What term is used to describe the document attached to an original contract?

    A. Addendum
    B. Signed agreement
    C. Requirements clause
    D. Terms and conditions

66. What refinancing method allows a borrower to acquire cash from the transaction?

    A. Cash flow
    B. Cash out refinance
    C. Cash on cash return
    D. Refinancing

67. Who oversees that code restrictions are followed and construction / renovation are done by licensed professionals?

    A. Contractor
    B. Department of Buildings
    C. Zoning board
    D. Architectural Review Board

68. What is the final stage of a real estate transaction?

    A. Closing
    B. Sale
    C. Final walk through
    D. Handing of the title

69. What is the percentage of the selling price that is usually earned by a real estate agent for facilitating the transaction?

    A. Bonus
    B. Commission
    C. Salary
    D. Rent

70. What is the name of fees paid to the lender at closing in exchange for a reduced interest rate?

    A. Mortgage
    B. Service fee
    C. Discount points
    D. Principal fee

71. Which Act was passed to protect against discrimination in borrowing?

    A. Equal Credit Opportunity Act
    B. Fair and Accurate Credit Transaction Act of 2003
    C. The Fair Credit Reporting Act
    D. Truth in Lending Act

72. What does the phrase "For Sale by Owner" mean?

    A. A sale is being facilitated by an agent
    B. Investors are open to receiving offers
    C. A property sale is being handled without a real estate agent
    D. All of the above

73. What is the name of the document used to summarize all the fees incurred by the lender and borrower during settlement of a loan?

    A. Financial statement
    B. Invoice
    C. IOU
    D. Settlement statement

74. Which entity determines the assessed value of a property?

    A. Building Inspector
    B. Municipal council
    C. Real estate agent
    D. Tax assessor

75. If a property is taxed at 40% with a tax levy of $88,000, what is its assessed value?

    A. $220,000
    B. $146,666
    C. $123,200
    D. None of the above

76. Which type of estate has rights to the property for an indefinite duration?

    A. List estate
    B. Estate for years
    C. Freehold estate
    D. Less-than-freehold estate

77. Which of the following is **not** an essential element of a deed?

    A. Signature of the grantee
    B. Date
    C. Identification of the grantor and grantee
    D. Adequate description of the property

78. What is a lessor?

    A. A person who leases real estate property from the owner of said property
    B. A person that makes a grant
    C. The owner of real estate who leases the property to another
    D. The person who transfers property by sale

79. What is the definition of a joint tenancy?

    A. When property is held by two or more parties
    B. When a third-party trust owns the property
    C. When the seller and the buyer both own the property
    D. When the property is inherited by a family member

80. What is the definition of a trust deed?

    A. The owner of the real estate property who leases the property to another
    B. A deed with limited or no warranties
    C. A deed that transfers property to a family member
    D. A document used when one party has taken out a loan from another party to purchase property

THIS IS THE END OF THE NATIONAL PORTION.

State Portion

1. All of the following applicants must complete education or training requirements prior to applying for a license **EXCEPT**

   A. Campground membership salespersons
   B. Cemetery salespersons
   C. Rental listing referral agents
   D. Time-share salespersons

2. In Pennsylvania, when do real estate salespersons' licenses expire?

   A. Two years from the date the license was issued
   B. Five years from the date the license was issued
   C. May 31 of every even-numbered year
   D. December 1 of the third year of licensure

3. In Pennsylvania, a salesperson or broker must do which of the following to renew their license?

   A. Prove U.S. citizenship
   B. Prove residence in Pennsylvania
   C. Active participation in real estate business
   D. Pay the appropriate renewal fee and complete 14 hours of continuing education

4. All of the following activities are included in the definition of the term "broker" **EXCEPT**

   A. Appraising real estate
   B. Managing real estate
   C. Performance of a market analysis
   D. Representing oneself as a real estate consultant or counselor

Practice Test 4 – State Portion

5. What is a builder-owner salesperson?

    A. A licensed real estate agent who works under a property constructor rather than a supervising broker
    B. Anyone engaged in in-house advertising for property developers
    C. A licensed real estate agent who specializes in commercial properties
    D. The legal term for an individual who is selling their own home without use of a licensed agent

6. Personal real estate assistants in Pennsylvania may do which of the following?

    A. Should always be licensed
    B. May deposit and withdraw funds from the broker's escrow account without being licensed
    C. If he or she is licensed, may host open houses for the public
    D. Can only be employed by the broker, instead of a salesperson

7. Through which law does the Pennsylvania Real Estate Commission gain the power to regulate the conduct of licensed agents?

    A. Pennsylvania Realty Codes
    B. Pennsylvania Real Estate Licensing and Registration Act
    C. Pennsylvania Service Regulations
    D. Federal Real Estate Licensing Act

8. An individual wants to obtain a Pennsylvania salesperson's license while holding a salesperson's license issued by another jurisdiction. Which of the following requirements must be met?

    A. Prior to the submission of a properly completed application, the salesperson's license issued by another jurisdiction must have been active for five years
    B. Must be a resident of Pennsylvania
    C. If the licensee is slow in processing the property transfer
    D. Must score more passing grade in Pennsylvania salesperson's license examination

Practice Test 4 – State Portion

9. The Pennsylvania Real Estate Commission must include at least one _____.

    A. Real estate broker
    B. Cemetery broker
    C. Attorney
    D. Member of a racial minority

10. If a real estate broker is advertising its services online, what must they include?

    A. Date of registration
    B. Licenses of all the broker's licensed agents
    C. Broker name as it appears on the license
    D. None of the above

11. A new buyer entered into a contract to buy a time-share interest in a unit from the developer. This new buyer has a right to cancel the contract?

    A. Within five days from the date the new buyer executed the contract
    B. Within two days from the date the buyer's attorney reviews the documents
    C. Any time
    D. Never

12. Who of the following is **not** exempt from the provisions of the Pennsylvania Real Estate License Act, and must hold a real estate license?

    A. Person who receives compensation from the sellers or landlords
    B. Someone who wants to sell his/her own property
    C. Person employed directly by owner of the property
    D. The bank manager responsible for all the real estate transactions

13. A real estate broker must keep records relating to real estate transactions for how long?

    A. One years from the date the property was listed
    B. Three years following consummation of the transaction
    C. Five years from the date the property was listed
    D. Indefinitely

14. Which of the following has authority to withdraw funds from the broker's escrow account for payments that are properly chargeable to the account?

    A. The finance audit officer
    B. Licensed employee who has been given written authority by the employing broker
    C. Unlicensed accountant or bookkeeper who is an employee of the broker
    D. Marketing manager directly hired by seller

15. An agent uses power of attorney to sign a legally binding document on behalf of their client. In Pennsylvania this situation _____.

    A. Constitutes designated agency
    B. Constitutes universal agency
    C. Is illegal unless the agent is also a licensed attorney
    D. Is always illegal

16. A housing discrimination charge must be filed with the Pennsylvania Human Relations Commission within

    A. 20 days
    B. 6 months
    C. 1 year
    D. 3 years

17. For engaging in real estate activities, a Pennsylvania real estate salesperson may lawfully collect compensation from which of the following?

    A. Respective employing broker only
    B. Directly from buyer
    C. From managing officer hired directly by buyer
    D. Pennsylvania Real Estate Commission

18. All of the following activities can be performed by a licensed salesperson for or on behalf of his or her employing broker **EXCEPT**

    A. Negotiate a loan on real estate
    B. Appraise single family property
    C. Buy or offer to buy real estate
    D. Lease commercial office building

19. The broker is certifying which of the following when he/she submits a salesperson's license application to the Pennsylvania Real Estate Commission?

    A. Broker will train and supervise the salesperson
    B. Being convicted criminal
    C. Salesperson is a resident of Pennsylvania
    D. Salesperson has not been arrested for any crime

20. An exclusive-right-to-buy contract in Pennsylvania:

    A. Is illegal
    B. Can continue for an indefinite time period
    C. Needs only the signature of the principal
    D. Must be mentioned in the buyer agency agreement

21. Representation agreements in Pennsylvania, that necessitate the buyer to pay a fee?

    A. Must be in written form
    B. Are not permitted
    C. Are not regulated under the license laws
    D. Are of no legal importance

22. Which of the following is **not** included in the Pennsylvania Real Estate Commission's rules regarding exclusive listing agreements?

    A. Listing agreement must state the fee the broker expects to earn
    B. Listing agreement must be accompanied by a qualified expert's report of the property's condition
    C. Seller should not be given a copy of the listing agreement
    D. Seller must receive a copy of the listing agreement after signing it

23. Which of the following is **not** included, as a provision in an agreement of sale, in a mortgage contingency?

    A. Type of mortgage
    B. Amount of the mortgage payment
    C. Maximum interest rate of the mortgage
    D. Final date for the buyer to obtain the mortgage

24. What is the difference between a broker and a broker associate?

    A. A broker must have three years' experience as a broker's salesperson while a broker associate must only have one
    B. A broker must be the only broker at their brokerage while a broker associate is part of a board of broker governance
    C. A broker is another term for broker of record while a broker associate is another term for a salesperson
    D. A broker runs their own brokerage while a broker associate is a licensed broker who works under another broker

25. What must newly licensed salespersons do with their licenses?

    A. They must send their license to be on file with the Pennsylvania Real Estate Commission
    B. They must display a photocopy of the license on the brokerage website
    C. Their broker of record must display their license prominently at the brokerage
    D. They must display their license in their personal office

26. In Pennsylvania, a tax will have to be paid on a transfer?

    A. Between parent and child
    B. Between government bodies
    C. Between educational institutions
    D. Of unimproved land to a developer

27. The maximum amount that a residential tenant has to pay as a security deposit in the first year of the lease, required by landlord is an amount?

    A. Not to exceed one month's rent
    B. Equivalent to two month's rent
    C. Equivalent to three month's rent
    D. Six-months commercial lease negotiated by a broker representing the building owner

28. An additional fee may be assessed by the Pennsylvania Real Estate Commission against licensees in order to increase the balance in the Real Estate Recovery Fund if?

    A. The number of new license fees during a biennial renewal period drops below $25,000
    B. During any one year, the amount paid from the fund exceeds $100,000
    C. Within three years the amount paid from the fund exceeds $500,000
    D. At the beginning of a biennial renewal period the balance in the fund is less than $200,000

29. Which is NOT a term for an account where brokers may deposit client earnest money?

    A. Escrow
    B. Trust
    C. Interest
    D. Custodial

30. What happens to the licensee when the court orders a payment to be made from the recovery fund owing to the improper activities of a licensee?

    A. The Pennsylvania Real Estate Commission takes no further action against the licensee
    B. Licensee's license is automatically revoked
    C. Licensee is subject to a fine of up to $1,000 but maintains an active license
    D. License is automatically suspended as of the date of payment

THIS IS THE END OF THE STATE PORTION.

Practice Test 4 – Answers

Answer Key – National Portion

1.	D	21.	B	41.	D	61.	B
2.	D	22.	A	42.	C	62.	D
3.	B	23.	B	43.	B	63.	A
4.	A	24.	A	44.	B	64.	B
5.	D	25.	B	45.	B	65.	A
6.	A	26.	D	46.	A	66.	B
7.	D	27.	A	47.	B	67.	B
8.	D	28.	A	48.	A	68.	A
9.	B	29.	C	49.	A	69.	B
10.	B	30.	C	50.	C	70.	C
11.	A	31.	C	51.	C	71.	A
12.	D	32.	D	52.	D	72.	C
13.	B	33.	B	53.	A	73.	D
14.	A	34.	B	54.	B	74.	D
15.	B	35.	D	55.	B	75.	A
16.	B	36.	B	56.	A	76.	C
17.	C	37.	A	57.	D	77.	A
18.	C	38.	C	58.	A	78.	C
19.	D	39.	A	59.	C	79.	A
20.	D	40.	D	60.	B	80.	D

1. **D) All of the above**

   Commercial property includes mixed use buildings (e.g. retail store on the first floor, residences above) office buildings, hotels, retail stores, multifamily houses, industrial warehouses, and more.

2. **D) Steering**

   Steering is the act of guiding prospective buyers to specified settlement areas based on race, religion and other discriminatory factors.

3. **B) Net lease**

   This is a lease where the tenant pays rent and part of utilities fee and property taxes. The landlord is tasked with paying the utility bills and property taxes that are not covered by the tenant. This lease is common in commercial real estate.

4. **A) Lis Pendens**

   This is a legal notice that a lawsuit concerning a real estate property is pending. Usually involves a property title or claims of ownership interest. Details of a property whose title is in question are required to be filed at the county record to notify future buyers and lenders.

Practice Test 4 – Answers

5. **D) Zoning Board of Appeals**

   The Zoning Board of Appeals is a board of select members that is given jurisdiction to hear and decide on appeals regarding zoning laws.

6. **A) Mortgage Banker**

   A mortgage banker is an individual who originates, closes and funds with his own funds or that of a company. Once a mortgage is originated it is either retained or sold to an investor. A mortgage banker has the power to approve or reject a mortgage and earns fees on the origination of a loan.

7. **D) Sheathing**

   Sheathing is a covering structure and acts as a case for the exterior of the home. Usually used to describe a boarding material that forms the roof, floor and walls. It provides a surface for other materials and strengthens weather resistance.

8. **D) Landlord**

   A security deposit is an amount equaling monthly rent that is paid to ensure rent will be paid and to cater for other responsibilities highlighted in the lease. Can also be used as security for unpaid rent and damages and is held onto by the landlord.

9. **B) Effective age**

   This is an estimate of a building age based on its utilities and the wear and tear. It could be the actual age or a little more or less than the actual age. This is dependent on maintenance, remodeling and removal of inadequacies. It is used to determine the remaining life of a building.

10. **B) Three years**

    Brokers are required by law to hold on to a copy of property files for a minimum of 3 years. This is to act as a proof in case of a dispute in the future. These include copies of all listings, deposit receipts, cancelled checks and trust records executed or obtained during the transaction.

11. **A) British Thermal Unit**

    Defined as the amount of heat required to raise the temperature of one pound of water by one-degree Fahrenheit. In the case of air conditioning, it is defined as the number of BTU per hour products that can be added or removed from the air.

Practice Test 4 – Answers

12. **D) Habendum clause**

    This is a legal agreement that involves the rights and interests of a property being transferred to a lessee. For a leased property there is a transfer of ownership and restrictions on the property. A purchased property is void of restrictions and only transfers ownership.

13. **B) Passive**

    This is an income source that requires little to no daily input in order to yield returns.

14. **A) Ground lease**

    This is a lease agreement where a tenant is allowed to develop a parcel of land during the lease period. On expiry of the lease, all improvements remain in the owner's custody. Land leases are often last between 50-99 with other agreement allowing for renewal.

15. **B) Building codes**

    These are a set of regulations that are put in place to ensure design, construction, alteration and maintenance of structures is done according to the state's requirements. They aim at safeguarding the health, safety and welfare of the occupants.

16. **B) $335,051**

    $325,000 / (1 - 0.03) = $335,051

17. **C) A fixture**

    A fixture is any physical property that is permanently attached to real property (usually land). Fixtures are treated as a part of real property. Examples of fixtures are ceiling fans and TV mounts.

18. **C) Offsite improvements**

    Offsite improvements are amenities that are not within the premise of the structure but are necessary to maximize the use of the property and ultimately increase the value of the property.

19. **D) Joint tenancy**

    Joint tenancy is a form of ownership in which several people own a property together, each with equal shares and rights. If one of the owners in a joint tenancy dies, that owner's share in the property is automatically passed to the remaining owners.

Practice Test 4 – Answers

20. **D) Preventive maintenance**

    In order to maintain tenants and an acceptable return on an investment, routine checks and repairs have to be done. These are done to safeguard against failing which may incur losses to the property manager that arise due to cost of replacement.

21. **B) CERCLA**

    The Comprehensive Environmental Response Compensation and Liability Act of 1980 was enacted in order to identify, investigate and facilitate cleanup of hazardous sites. The act is currently administered by the Environmental Protection Agency.

22. **A) A shared tenancy in which each holder has a distinct, separately transferable interest**

    This type of ownership is characterized by ownership between two or more people who can have either equal or unequal shares. Unlike a joint tenancy, if an owner dies, the person's share is passed to his/her heirs and not distributed to the remaining owners.

23. **B) Cash flow**

    This is the amount of profit retained after paying off all operating costs and repurposing amounts made in dividends for use in future repairs. To be able to profit from an investment, one must maintain a positive cash flow.

24. **A) A lien that arises without the property owner's consent**

    Involuntary liens are placed by government facilities for unpaid taxes.

25. **B) Homestead property**

    Homestead laws are laws that exist to ensure to protect owners from losing their home equity while filing for bankruptcy. Homestead property enables an individual to declare a portion of property as homestead to avoid forced sale.

26. **D) Special agent**

    This is an agent engaged to perform a specific duty for a client. Their authority is limited to that particular task that translates in the expiry of the contract once the task is completed.

27. **A) Bundle of rights**

    These are legal rights that are granted to a property buyer which include right to possession, control, exclusion, enjoyment and disposition. A property owner is automatically granted the bundle of rights. In a commercial property, different rights can be assigned to different parties.

Practice Test 4 — Answers

28. **A) $1,000**

Violation of license laws may result in suspension of a license or a fine of not more than $1,000 paid to the Department of State. A reprimand is given together with the fine.

29. **C) 39 years**

After 39 years a commercial property is eligible for applying for value loss by depreciation in order to reduce property taxes levied

30. **C) Proration**

Proration occurs during corporate action to ensure all shareholders are treated fairly and a company does not deviate from its original target. Shareholders are offered equity or cash and required to elect one. Once the election is done, shareholders are compensated and if the shares or cash are not enough to satisfy the election each shareholder gets their due in both equity and cash.

31. **C) 7.48 gallons**

32. **D) Operating statement**

An operating statement is a financial statement that is done monthly and annually to document the expenses incurred and revenue gained. From the statement one can calculate the net profit or loss within the period.

33. **B) Condop**

This is a real estate building where the housing units are divided into co-op residential units and condos. They offer more flexible rules than a co-op. Condo units are retained or sold separately by the developer.

34. **B) General Agent**

This is an agent that is mandated to represent the principal in more than one affair.

35. **D) Usury**

These are laws that are laws set in place to protect borrowers from abusive lending such as imposing unusually high interest rates. Lenders usually target with little knowledge on the traditional loan system. An APR is usually set to protect buyers from being exploited by lenders.

Practice Test 4 – Answers

36. **B) Leasehold**

This is a title on a property being leased and scheduled payments are made throughout the term of the lease. Improvements made within the property are either expensed or capitalized depending on their values.

37. **A) Mortgage**

A mortgage is a voluntary lien taken out to raise funds to buy a property. The lien is entered willingly and therefore possession of the property remains with the debtor.

38. **C) Tenancy in sufferance**

In this case, a tenant is granted the privilege to live within the premise before landlord decides to ask the tenant to vacate. Terms of the original lease must be met during this period of time. This type of tenancy can only be terminated by a written notice given not less than 30 days before the tenant is expected to move out.

39. **A) Yes**

There are no laws restricting a real estate salesperson from working multiple jobs.

40. **D) Private investors and government agencies that buy and sell real estate mortgages**

This is where home loans and servicing rights are bought within the market. Once a home loan is obtained, it is underwritten, financed and services by a lending facility. A lending facility sells loans to the secondary mortgage market in order to replenish loaning money.

41. **D) Rights granted to a property owner on the vertical space above the property**

The air space is subject to reasonable use by neighboring buildings and aircrafts. Like with property, air rights can be leased or sold.

42. **C) Co-broking**

This is a situation where two or more agents that are involved in the same the same transaction agree to work together in order to meet the needs of both parties. In this case, the agents are legally required to act in the best interest of the clients.

43. **B) Lease assignment**

A lease assignment is a legal arrangement where the landlord allows a tenant to assign another tenant to lease the apartment. The tenant is responsible for paying rent and utility fees directly to the landlord. In the case of a lease assignment, the previous tenant is held accountable for defaults in unpaid bills by the assignee.

Practice Test 4 – Answers

44. **B) $2,000**

    ($200,000 * 0.12) / 12 = $2,000

45. **B) Closing costs**

    These are the extra costs that are usually incurred by a home buyer on top the agreed upon price. They usually include title insurance, attorney fees and lender fees. These costs are negotiable but commonly paid by buyers.

46. **A) Common charges**

    These are the monthly charges that are imposed on condo and condop tenants to cover common charges and amenities. They are usually cover maintenance of shared spaces and operation expenses of a building.

47. **B) Debt to income ratio**

    This is a way lenders use to calculate the ability of a borrower to manage the monthly payments required in the settlement plan. Borrowers with a higher ratio have been established to experience struggles in meeting the monthly payments. 43% has been determined to be the highest ratio that can be offered credit.

48. **A) Down payment**

    A down payment is an amount paid by the buyer to the seller to secure the property. A down payment is usually paid from the buyer's savings. Contrary to common belief, there is no set percentage of down payment that should be placed on a property

49. **A) Money deposited by the buyer to the seller to show interest in the purchase of a home**

    This amount is deposited to give the buyer time to look into the title, sanction an appraisal and conduct an inspection of the property. This money can be returned to the buyer only in the case of a contract breach.

50. **C) Escrow**

    This arrangement involves a third party that is neutral to the transaction. Usually used to secure payment in an account that can only be released on meeting of all the terms of the agreement. An escrow account is often used in transactions that involve large amounts of money such as real estate. A listing agent open an account and once the terms are signed upon by both the buyer and the seller, the deal is closed.

Practice Test 4 – Answers

51. **C) Notice of termination**

    This is a notice given to a tenant to end tenancy stating the reason for termination of tenancy, the date by which the tenant is required to vacate the premise and the legal implication of refusing to move.

52. **D) Notice to quit**

    This is a notice given by the landlord regarding someone living in the home as a squatter. The notice usually states that the tenant is required to vacate the property within 10 days and the implications of failing to do so.

53. **A) Notice of cessation**

    This is notice given by the contractor by the contractee to state that no work regarding construction has been done for a specified period of time. This notice is given in order to begin mechanical liens compensation.

54. **B) Home inspection**

    They are an important part of the real estate transaction as one is able to identify the condition of the property being bought. Inspection of facilities such as plumbing, fixtures and foundation condition comes in handy in determining the value of the property.

55. **B) Convertible ARM**

    This is a mortgage plan that allows an individual to benefit from the falling interest rates with the option of switching to a fixed-rate payment plan at a small fee. This switch can be made within the second to fifth year of the mortgage payment period.

56. **A) Delinquency**

    This is a situation that arises where a borrower that is legally bound with the responsibility to make necessary payments on a loan or a bond interest foregoes paying the loan. Delinquency usually results in penalties depending on the type of loan and reasons behind failed payments.

57. **D) Federal Housing Administration**

    This is United States Agency whose goal is to enable low income individual acquire mortgage loans. The agency approves and insures the lenders. An FHA loan requires a loan down payment and a credit score of at least 580.

58. **A) Consumer Financial Protection Bureau**

    This is a regulatory agency that is tasked with the responsibility of overseeing the products and services offered to consumers by financial institutions. In the event of mishandling of a consumer, a complaint is filed to the CFPB for resolution.

Practice Test 4 – Answers

59. **C) Multiple Listing Service**

    This is a system employed by real estate broker that allows them to view each other's listings. Sharing the database amongst a group of brokers enables brokers to identify buyers for properties they are engaged in.

60. **B) Home warranty**

    This is a contract made to ensure the cost of maintaining a household are met. It is put in place as a legal assurance that the property is fit for its intended purpose and meets the expectations of the buyer. It is usually taken to protect against expensive home repairs.

61. **B) Escalation clause**

    This is a contract that allows a buyer to set a selling price but any offers higher than the stated price will automatically lead to an increase in the set price. This gives sellers an option to outbid each other and help in making the decision for the sale price.

62. **D) Notice of intent**

    This is a non-binding proposal between a buyer and seller of a property to negotiate terms of a real estate transaction. It is usually detailed and lays key points on the weight of the transaction. It is usually used to determine the seriousness of the prospective buyer on the property.

63. **A) Appreciation**

    This is the increase in the value of an asset over a period of time. It usually occurs due to increased demand or weakening supply.

64. **B) Biweekly mortgage**

    This is a mortgage that requires a principal and interest payment plan every two weeks. It usually has a reduced interest rate throughout the lifespan of the loan.

65. **A) Addendum**

    This is an attached document that is usually included as part of the contract during the preparation. It can act as an informal explanatory attachment or to indicate other requirements of the contract that have not been included in the main attachment.

66. **B) Cash out refinance**

    This is where a homeowner refinances a mortgage for more than its value and withdraws the difference amount as cash. It is only possible to borrowers with a 20% equity on their mortgage.

Practice Test 4 – Answers

67. **B) Department of Buildings**

    In order to ensure that building codes are adhered to and construction and renovations are done by professionals, a building permit is required for any building or renovation project. A building permit is a go ahead issued by local government to a contractor to construct or remodel a building. It is issued to ensure that building codes are adhered to and standards are maintained.

68. **A) Closing**

    This is the final stage of a real estate transaction. At this point, the date where contract becomes active is agreed on. On the closing date, the property is legally transferred from the seller to the buyer.

69. **B) Commission**

    This is the percentage earned by a real estate agent for effort placed in facilitating the transaction. It is usually between 5-6% of the sales price and is paid by the seller on closing. It is usually split between the buyer's and seller's agent.

70. **C) Discount points**

    Also referred to as mortgage points, these are fees paid directly to a lender by a homebuyer at closing time. They are usually paid in exchange for lower interest rates reducing monthly payments on the mortgage.

71. **A) Equal Credit Opportunity Act**

    This act was enacted in 1974 and rules it unlawful for lenders to discriminate against loan applicants based on gender, race, age and religion.

72. **C) A property sale is being handled without a real estate agent**

    This phrase is used to declare that a property sale is being handled without a real estate agent. While using real estate agents to facilitate sale, some home sellers would rather avoid agents in order to save on the amount spent on commission. In this case the seller must disclose that they are not using an agent.

73. **D) Settlement statement**

    This is a document that is usually used to summarize expenses incurred during a loan translation and varies according to loan types. It is usually part of the closing package that must be reviewed and signed by the borrower when closing a loan. A comprehensive settlement statement is legally required for every loan.

Practice Test 4 – Answers

74. **D) Tax assessor**

    An official whose responsibility is to determine the value of each taxable property in a region.

75. **A) $220,000**

    $88,000 / 0.4 = $220,000

76. **C) Freehold estate**

    An estate that has exclusive rights of the property for an undefined length of time. The three types of freehold estates are fee simple absolute, fee simple defeasible and life estate.

77. **A) Signature of the grantee**

    The grantee does not need to sign a deed. A deed needs to be in writing, must be signed by the grantor, the grantor must have the legal capacity to transfer the property, the grantor and grantee must be identified, the property must be described adequately, the deed must be legally delivered to the grantee and the grantee must accept the deed.

78. **C) The owner of real estate who leases the property to another**

    A person who grants a lease to someone else. This person is the owner of the real estate and leases it a lessee through an agreement.

79. **A) When property is held by two or more parties**

    It is an agreement in which two or more people own a property with equal rights and obligations. Joint tenancy is typically entered at the same time and through a deed. If one of the owners were to die their portion of the property would automatically pass to the survivors.

80. **D) A document used when one party has taken out a loan from another party to purchase property**

    It represents an agreement between the borrower and the lender in which the property is held in a trust managed by a third party until the borrower pays off the loan. The legal title of the property is transferred to the third party to hold. Trust deeds are used in place of mortgages in numerous states.

Practice Test 4 – Answers

Answer Key – State Portion

1.	B	21.	A
2.	C	22.	B
3.	D	23.	B
4.	A	24.	D
5.	A	25.	C
6.	C	26.	D
7.	B	27.	B
8.	A	28.	A
9.	B	29.	C
10.	C	30.	D
11.	A		
12.	A		
13.	B		
14.	B		
15.	B		
16.	C		
17.	A		
18.	B		
19.	A		
20.	D		

1. **B) Cemetery salespersons**

   There is no education requirement or exam required for a cemetery salesperson (541).

2. **C) May 31 of every even-numbered year**

   Salesperson and broker licenses all expire on the last day of May in even-numbered years and must be renewed on or before June 1.

3. **D) Pay the appropriate renewal fee and complete 14 hours of continuing education**

   Renewal fees established by the commission must be paid. (407(a)). Commission rules (35.382) require a broker or salesperson to complete 14 hours of commission approved continuing education as a condition precedent to the renewal of a current license.

4. **A) Appraising real estate**

   The State Board of Certified Real Estate Appraisers regulates appraisal activities, rather than the Pennsylvania Real Estate Commission.

Practice Test 4 – Answers

5. **A) A licensed real estate agent who works under a property constructor rather than a supervising broker**

   A builder-owner salesperson works directly for a builder or developer, rather than a broker. Building-owner salespersons must still be licensed in order to legally work as a real estate salesperson.

6. **C) If he or she is licensed, may host open houses for the public**

   Only licensed employees of the broker may hold open houses for the public and withdraw funds from the brokers escrow account.

7. **B) Pennsylvania Real Estate Licensing and Registration Act**

   The Pennsylvania Real Estate Licensing and Registration Act allows the Pennsylvania Real Estate commission to license agents and regulate their behavior, including holding disciplinary hearings, suspending or revoking licenses, and, when appropriate, referring a case to civil or criminal court.

8. **A) Prior to the submission of a properly completed application, the salesperson's license issued by another jurisdiction must have been active for five years**

   An individual holding a salesperson's license issued by another jurisdiction must prove that this license has been active within five years prior to submission of the application (35.223(b)).

9. **B) Cemetery broker**

   The Pennsylvania Real Estate Commission must include at least five licensed real estate brokers and one cemetery broker

10. **C) Broker name as it appears on the license**

    The official name of the broker printed on the license must be visible on any form of web advertising.

11. **A) Within five days from the date the new buyer executed the contract**

    A purchaser has the right to cancel the purchase of a time-share interest until midnight of the fifth day following the date on which the purchaser executed the purchase contract (609 (a)).

12. **A) Person who receives compensation from the sellers or landlords**

    An individual who undertakes to promote the sale, exchange, purchase, or rental of real estate or who represents himself to be a real estate consultant, counselor, agent, or finder is required to hold a broker's license (201(1)).

Practice Test 4 – Answers

13. **B) Three years following consummation of the transaction**

    License law requires the broker to keep records relating to a real estate transaction for three years following processing of the transaction (604 (a)(6)).

14. **B) Licensed employee who has been given written authority by the employing broker**

    The employing broker may give a licensed employee written authority to withdraw funds from the escrow account (35.325 (b)).

15. **B) Constitutes universal agency**

    An uncommon situation in residential real estate, universal agency (unlike special or general agency) allows the licensed agent to act as the client in all or most matters, pursuant to the contract. This represents the broadest power a licensed agent can take on behalf of a client.

16. **C) 1 year**

    Complaints must be filed within one year of the alleged violation.

17. **A) Respective employing broker only**

    License law prohibits a salesperson or associate broker from accepting compensation from anyone other than his or her employing broker (604 (a)(12)).

18. **B) Appraise single family property**

    The definition of a salesperson does not allow a licensed salesperson to engage in appraisal activity (201).

19. **A) Broker will train and supervise the salesperson**

    In order to be licensed as a salesperson, the candidate must submit a license application with a sworn statement from the broker certifying that the broker will actively supervise and train the applicant (35.223 (a)).

20. **D) Must be mentioned in the buyer agency agreement**

    606.1 (b)(l) requires the nature of the service to be provided must be set forth in a written agreement between the consumer and the licensee. Section 608.1 establishes requirements for the written agreement. An exclusive-right-to-buy contract must be in written form and contain a specific termination date.

21. **A) Must be in written form**

    608.1 establishes that any agreement between a broker and a principal whereby the consumer is obligated to pay a fee must be in writing and signed by the consumer.

Practice Test 4 – Answers

22. **B) Listing agreement must be accompanied by a qualified expert's report of the property's condition**

    A qualified expert's report covering property condition is not required when a seller lists property for sale with a broker.

23. **B) Amount of the mortgage payment**

    The amount of the mortgage payment is not included in mortgage contingency clauses (35.333 (b)).

24. **D) A broker runs their own brokerage while a broker associate is a licensed broker who works under another broker**

    A broker associate is a fully licensed broker who does not wish to or is not ready to run their own brokerage. Broker associates work under other brokers, who are the brokers of record for their brokerages.

25. **C) Their broker of record must display their license prominently at the brokerage**

    The broker of record of the brokerage must display their license, as well as the licenses of all their broker associates and salespersons, prominently at the brokerage's physical office.

26. **D) Of unimproved land to a developer**

    A transfer of unimproved land is subject to transfer taxes. The state tax is 1% of the full consideration paid for the property.

27. **B) Equivalent to two month's rent**

    Pennsylvania law limits the amount landlords can charge as a security deposit. During the first year of tenancy, the maximum is an amount equal to two months' rent.

28. **A) The number of new license fees during a biennial renewal period drops below $25,000**

    The Real Estate Recovery Fund was created to provide a vehicle by which consumers who have obtained a final judgment against a licensee may recover compensation from the commission. Application to the fund may be made only after all reasonable remedies available have been exhausted (803).

29. **C) Interest**

    Escrow, trust, or custodial accounts are accounts controlled by brokers to hold client earnest money and any other client funds that need to be held in escrow. Most custodial accounts do not accrue interest. Brokers may only deposit personal or operating money in a trust account to cover fees and keep the account open; brokers may never withdraw money from the account for their own purposes.

Practice Test 4 – Answers

30. **D) License is automatically suspended as of the date of payment**

The license is automatically suspended as of the effective date of payment when payment is made from the recovery fund. In order for the licensee to have the license reinstated, the licensee must repay the full amount plus interest at the rate of 10% per year (803 (f)).

Resources

3.1 Finding a broker

Now that you've passed the exam, it's time to officially become an agent! Below is a list of companies and their websites to help you expedite your job search and help you start your journey in selling your first Pennsylvania property!

CBRE – http://www.cbre.us/people-and-offices/corporate-offices/philadelphia
JLL – https://www.us.jll.com/en/locations/northeast/philadelphia
Newmark Knight Frank – http://www.ngkf.com
Colliers International – https://www2.colliers.com/en/United-States/Cities/Philadelphia
Marcus & Millichap – https://www.marcusmillichap.com/properties/regional-investment-markets/metro-areas/philadelphia
Cushman & Wakefield – http://www.cushmanwakefield.com
NAI Geis Realty Group – https://corenyc.com
The Flynn Co. – http://flynnco.com
Metro Commercial Real Estate Inc. – https://www.metrocommercial.com
Binswanger Management Corp.– https://www.binswanger.com
Jackson Cross Partners – https://www.jacksoncross.com
NAI Mertz – http://www.naimertz.com
MSC Retail – https://mscretail.com
Avison Young – https://www.avisonyoung.com
Equity Retail Brokers Inc. – https://www.equityretailbrokers.com

Resources

Patterson-Woods Commercial Properties – https://www.pattersonwoods.com
Rittenhouse Realty Advisors – https://www.rittenhouserealty.com
MPN Realty Inc. – http://mpnrealty.com
SSH Real Estate – http://sshrealestate.com
Tactix Real Estate Advisors – http://tactix.com
Wolf Commercial Real Estate (WCRE) – https://wolfcre.com
Savills – https://www.savills.us
HFF – https://www.hfflp.com
Cresa – https://www.cresa.com
Gola Corporate Real Estate – https://gola.com
Stockton Real Estate Advisors – https://stocktonrea.com/

3.2 Interviewing

Congratulations! You did get the interview. Now, just a little work and you can ace it!

First, start by going to all of the social media pages associated with your potential employer. Focus on several interesting things that they do and specialize in. Look at which type of listings they are showing on their pages and what types of neighborhoods they appear for listings. Look up the particular broker you are interviewing with and go to his/her LinkedIn page and learn more about her/him.

While you're looking at your potential employer's social media pages, take a look at your own. Are there any posts on your Facebook or other social media sites that need to be removed? Employers are looking at your pages. Anything inappropriate needs to go!

Real estate is all about creating a network of potential clients who trust that what you're selling to them will meet their needs. This means you must understand to differentiate between a client looking to buy a house to raise their newborn and a client who is looking for long term appreciation.

Try simulating cold calls by opening up random properties on Zillow or Trulia, studying them for 2 minutes, and then trying to sell your friend on these properties. They will most likely be asking similar questions to actual prospective buyers or sellers, so it's a very useful exercise in preparing yourself for the mock cold call during the interview.

In addition, study the geography of your broker's city to make sure you don't go in completely blind. Get familiar with the prices and trends in those areas and even take a tour. Drive or walk around and know the neighborhood like the back of your hand so you can impress the employer

On the day of the interview choose your outfit carefully. You should wear some type of suit and make sure your shoes are in good condition. Ask a friend to give you input on the clothes that make you look the most professional. Make sure you brushed your teeth, and your hair is neatly styled. Make sure you don't smell of smoke as most workplaces are smoke-free. No perfume or cologne – your new office may be perfume free. Never chew gum! You will not get the job!

When you arrive at the interview, always make sure to greet the receptionist. Every person you meet at your potential future employer is important! Make a good impression.

Resources

When you land the interview, it's important to have certain answers prepared to more commonly asked questions. First, let's look at general types of questions that you may be asked at any type of interview:

1. Tell me about yourself. This is not the time to talk about everything that happened to you from birth. This is an opportunity to show off a certain drive or characteristic or hobby that is special and helps to explain why you are seeking that particular job. For example, did you participate in a lot of team sports or a lot of clubs in high school or college? Did you work on volunteer projects that required you to meet a lot of new people of all ages and work with them and/or help them? The interviewer has your resume (Always bring extras with you!), so you do not have to spout off all of your previous education and positions. Devote just a sentence or two to that part of your answer.

2. What are your greatest strengths and weaknesses? This is a very tricky question. We all know our strengths; winning personality, gets along with everyone, good at math, good at negotiating, etc., but what about our weaknesses? Well, you certainly want to be honest but now isn't the time to confess all. Choose one. Do you take too long sometimes on a project because you want every detail to be perfect? Do you sometimes want to do something completely by yourself, but you really would be better off asking others for help? These are just two examples of weaknesses that won't sound like you are unprepared for your new job.

3. Where do you see yourself in 5 years? This seems pretty straightforward but be careful. The person interviewing you could be a manager. It is best not to say that you want his/her job. Instead, it may be better to say, I see myself expanding into new roles, doing what I do better, expanding my client base, becoming more successful, continuing my real estate education, and similar phrases.

4. Why did you choose our Company? Everyone asks this question. If you haven't gone to the Company's website, don't go to the interview. You should know everything about the Company and the local office where you are interviewing. You should know which type of real estate they specialize in, how long it's been in business, any recent mergers or expansions, the physical area it is licensed to practice in, and as much as you find on their website and Facebook page and other social media.

5. Why should I hire you and not the next person? This is your moment in the spotlight. Don't just say "pick me!!". Here is a sample: "All of my life, I have enjoyed working with people; when I worked at X company or volunteered at Y organization, I was able to get along with all types of people from children to the elderly. I also have been on teams or worked on teams, and I enjoy it greatly. I like to help people, and there is no bigger purchase than a home. I believe that I have the people skills and the real estate knowledge that I need to be a successful addition to your Company.

6. Why are you leaving your current job? This is not the moment to say how much you dislike your current manager or co-worker. Always be positive at your interview. You can talk about the lack of advancement opportunities, a salary freeze, future layoff being expected, change in your current employer's office location, or some other concrete reason. You can even say that you don't feel all of your skills are being utilized, and you want to use your new knowledge every day in your job.

Resources

7. Give me an example of a situation where you used teamwork to accomplish your goal. Even if you only work by yourself at your current job, look back to previous jobs and have the answer ready. If you don't have a job that matches, think about your volunteer activities at your children's school or at a community center or retirement village.

8. Would you rather work by yourself or as part of a team? This may be a good one to answer with a bit of vagueness. You can say that it depends on what the assignment might be. Do you have to give a major presentation to a commercial client? That might be a great time to ask for input and help as needed. Do you have to write a simple analysis of a problem? Maybe you feel more comfortable completing this on your own. You might want to say that it is very important to ask for feedback from co-workers and managers on projects and on small assignments when you have questions or reach a dead end.

9. What type of manager do you prefer? Do you prefer to work independently or to have more direction? This is always a tricky one as well. Make sure, once again, that you don't diss any of your former managers. A good response would be that you expect some direction from your manager. You feel that you know generally when you need help and would be sure to ask your manager for direction at those times. Also, you welcome all constructive feedback. It is very important to show that you are open to learning and open to change.

10. Why do you have gaps on your resume? Make sure you know the answer in advance to this question. Were you raising a family, taking care of an elderly parent, moving across the country due to a partner relocation, volunteering, etc.? Whatever it is, make sure to answer this one without any hesitation and move on.

11. What is customer service? Be careful with this one. There are two types of customers – internal and external. Everyone you work with in your office is an internal customer; others are external. The same level of consideration should be given to both internal and external customers. Speak about how important it is to answer questions, do tasks that are needed, go above and beyond the average effort, and ask for help if you don't know the answers.

12. Are you organized? No one wants to admit they are disorganized. If you are going into real estate where there are mounds of paperwork and so many different elements to keep track with, let's assume that every person interviewing for this position must be organized!

13. What do you do when several people give you tasks to do, and it is clear to you that you will not be able to finish them on time?

14. Tell me about a time when you went above and beyond what was required? Hopefully, this will be an easy one to answer. Think about a suggestion you made to your manager to take on more work when a fellow employee was out sick or a time when you thought the presentation needed a special PowerPoint and you produced it.

15. Tell me about a time you had to deal with a difficult person and how you managed to diffuse the situation? You really need to think about this one in advance. If you can't think of a difficult person in your professional life, think about a friend of a friend or someone else. Always acknowledge a difficult person's feelings and avoid arguing about strong opinions that impact an issue that isn't really that important.

Resources

16. If we offer you the position, how much notice do you have to give to your current employer? Be prepared to know the answer to this one. If you say that you can leave tomorrow, your future employer may not be pleased. It shows that you are not being loyal to your current employer by leaving them in the lurch. Two weeks is standard practice, but if you have a contract, be sure to read it.

Then, you will be asked more specific questions that are relevant to the real estate industry or this particular job. These include but are not limited to:

1. Why do you want to work in the real estate business?
2. This is a commission-based business, which means there is no ceiling to how much you can earn, but it also means there is no floor either. Are you open to this?
3. Let's go through a mock cold call together. I'll be the buyer, and you'll be the seller's agent.
4. How would you sell a property in a neighborhood you've never been to before?
5. A couple is looking to buy their first home. What kind of houses would you suggest?
6. A seasoned investor is looking for investment properties. By coincidence, the Independence Hall is for sale and you are the seller's agent. Pitch it to them.
7. A retiree is looking to sell their house. He is unsure about whether it's a good time to sell it. Explain to them why it is a good time to put the property on the market.

Be prepared to answer technical questions you may have studied for your exam such as:

1. What is the difference between a joint tenancy and a tenancy by the entireties?
2. What is the difference between a cooperative and a condominium?
3. Why is title insurance important?
4. Why would a buyer agree to lease back to a seller?
5. What are the duties of a buyer's agent?
6. What is a tax credit opposed to a tax deduction?
7. What is an easement?
8. Why would someone want to partition property, and what does this mean?
9. When would there be a lien on real estate?
10. What happens at settlement?
11. Why would a homeowner agree to finance a second mortgage for the buyer?

At the end of an interview, the interviewer will always ask if you have any questions. It is never a good idea to say, "No"! Here are some suggestions:

1. If I work here full time, what would be a range of the commissions I could expect in the first year?
2. What type of commission structure is there? Are commissions paid immediately upon closing? What types of fees am I required to pay out-of-pocket? Do I pay any advertising, computer, or other fees?
3. How often would I normally be assigned floor duty? If I answer the phone while on floor duty, do I get that listing?
4. How many open houses would I normally attend a month?
5. What is your hiring process timewise?
6. Do you pay for continuing education?

7. Although I know there isn't a truly "typical" day, what kinds of activities will I be performing during my first few weeks on the job?
8. When I attend my first settlement, will someone more senior come with me to the closing?
9. Will I attend all of the inspections for my listings?
10. What are the types of problems that arise at settlement?
11. Do you give out a list of mortgage brokers to clients?
12. How many people work in this office?
13. Is there coordination with other nearby offices – both this brand and others?
14. Do you provide a list of mortgage brokers to the buyer?

When you are finished with your interview, make sure to thank the interviewer, ask for her/his card, and thank the receptionist before you leave. Every impression counts! When you arrive home, if you really do want to work at that office, within 24 hours write a short email thank you note to your interviewer. If you don't hear back within a week, you can send a brief follow-up e-mail expressing your continuing interest in the position.

Made in the USA
Middletown, DE
27 May 2023